THE CRAZY QUILT OF LIFE

2/21/13

To Sherry —

One of only a few friends who knew mom & what a sweet & loving person she was to us all.

Love & Blessings from Zida-Ann & her loving grandaughter; Margaret Ann Parker

Proverbs 3

THE CRAZY QUILT OF LIFE

Lida Beaty-Jackson

Inspiring Voices®
A Service of **Guideposts**

Copyright © 2012 Margaret Ann Parker

All rights reserved. No part of this book may be used or reproduced by any means, graphic, electronic, or mechanical, including photocopying, recording, taping or by any information storage retrieval system without the written permission of the publisher except in the case of brief quotations embodied in critical articles and reviews.

Inspiring Voices books may be ordered through booksellers or by contacting:

Inspiring Voices
1663 Liberty Drive
Bloomington, IN 47403
www.inspiringvoices.com
1-(866) 697-5313

Because of the dynamic nature of the Internet, any web addresses or links contained in this book may have changed since publication and may no longer be valid. The views expressed in this work are solely those of the author and do not necessarily reflect the views of the publisher, and the publisher hereby disclaims any responsibility for them.

Any people depicted in stock imagery provided by Thinkstock are models, and such images are being used for illustrative purposes only.

Certain stock imagery © Thinkstock.

ISBN: 978-1-4624-0456-8 (sc)
ISBN: 978-1-4624-0455-1 (e)

Library of Congress Control Number: 2012923343

Printed in the United States of America

Inspiring Voices rev. date: 12/13/2012

For Lida and all of the colorful ancestors that have been stitched together to create the remarkable quilt that is our family.

Lida and her father, David

I will praise You, for I am fearfully and wonderfully made; Marvelous are Your works, and that my soul knows very well.
—Psalm 139:14

CONTENTS

Introduction xi
The Beginning of a Journey 1
Building the Soddy 7
Neighbors on the Prairie 10
The School Debate 14
An Early American Classroom 18
Christmastime 21
Family Life 27
Independence Day 34
The Stories of Sam and Mart 37
A Land of Extremes 40
Storms and Fire 44
Hard Times Call for Harder Work 49
Home Remedies 54
Beauty from the Dirt 58
Old Cleopatra and Cheap Jim 62
Time for a Change 65
Jetmore 69
Osawatomie 74
High School 78
Graduation and Pike's Peak 82
The Most Exciting News 87
Soap, Spice, and Missionaries 92
Herbert Pearce 94

Larned	98
On to Washington	105
A Farewell	111
Epilogue	113
Extra Stories about Lida Ann's Ancestors	114
Samuel Alley	123
Cyrus and Charity Nelson	127
The Benediction of Samuel Alley	130

INTRODUCTION

Each person in a family tree is like a beautifully woven piece of fabric. Every miraculous life connects over time to become a unique and sometimes crazy quilt. At first, only two or three pieces are cut out. But as the next generation is born, new patterns, new colors, and new textures are sewn onto the original pieces, adding to it and making it more magnificent. And knowing about the quilt of a family tree has the power to keep the whole family warm.

Families are timelines that reach far back into history. Ancestors pass on wonderful gifts and talents down the line. To know the history of our ancestors is truly a blessing, and it has the power to strengthen one's faith in God.

The author of this diary, Lida Beaty-Jackson, was extremely fortunate to know so much about her brave and colorful relatives. And now her personal account of life and some of those stories are being passed on to you.

THE BEGINNING OF A JOURNEY

Lida, her mother, and her sister Minnie Elizabeth.

I am not certain when Grandfather Alley moved with his family from Decatur County to Tipton County Indiana, about a hundred miles to the north, or why, but I am fairly sure it was to secure bounty land in return for his army service. They settled near the village of Sharpsville. Mother was in her teens. There, at age nineteen, she met and married my father, David Ephraim Beaty. (He never went farther than the E. when writing his middle name.) They were married on January 7, 1875. Father was just past twenty-two.

Kansas was a magical word in the 1880s. It had a magnetic power that drew people from nearly every state east of the Mississippi River. Not just the young men but the middle-aged and old as well. Leaving behind the home grounds, which their fathers and grandfathers had wrested from the wilderness, making it safe and pleasant to live in such places, entire families turned their faces toward the vast, alluring, and untried West. It was a mass movement, and such migrations have a strange power. There is a hurry to get ready. Goods are quickly turned into cash—usually at a value much less than the goods are worth—and those precious possessions that are too heavy to take are left with relatives. On the day of departure, there are quick and tearful good-byes. The ones leaving say, "We're off."

Off to what? To many people, the dream proved to be a deceptive mirage. To the others who stuck it out, it was a journey of hardship and loneliness—one defeat after another in their conflict with the weather until at last victory, in some form, was achieved. If the victory was not directly for them, it was for their children, who would live and adjust to the new environment.

In September 1882, my father set forth with my mother, my sister Elizabeth, and myself. I was only ten months old. We halted in Linn County, just across the Missouri boundary into Kansas. Here, my father rented rich land along the Big Sugar Creek and went to work. During the first year there, aunts and uncles and their families followed us, along with Grandmother and Grandfather Alley. They all found it pleasant there, with good land to farm, good fishing, and good neighbors. But the winds of the rolling, treeless plains farther west kept up their siren songs, and my father became restless; he wanted to continue on.

On March 22, 1884, my dear little grandmother, Eliza Pumphrey Alley, went to her last rest at only fifty-two years of age. They buried her at Wesley Chapel near the village of Wallstreet. Her grave is marked, and someday I hope to visit it.

There had been a very strong bond between my grandmother and my mother. So now that Grandmother was gone, Mother gave more heed to my father's insistence that we move farther west. Accordingly, in the fall of 1884, Father and Mother climbed to the spring seat of the heavily loaded covered wagon and again took the westward trail. Mother, who was leaving her family, the grave of her mother and was expecting a new baby before many weeks, was desolate. However, my father had the vigor and vision of a young man; he was thrilled and confident of a bright future. By nature he was the very soul of cheerfulness and optimism; he continued to be until the end of his long life. He was a keen observer, alert on both political and economic matters, and with his great humor, he was able to make many friends, both young and old. He always made time to chat with anyone. Mother was different, though. Modest and retiring, she made fewer friends. But when she made them, they would be sincere ones. As the horses pulled the wagon westward, Father was excited for the opportunity ahead. But Mother was leaving all of her world behind.

Father planned to go two hundred miles west to the town of Stafford, where we would remain for the winter. Then, with the return of spring, we would go another hundred miles where we would stake a claim. Stafford is the first place that I can remember. I was three years old that November, and there are four things that I can recall quite clearly from that time: the odor of a red-lined overshoe; seeing a crock full of pressed meat; fearing that Sophia Crawford would cut off my ears if I marked on the wall anymore; and the most unusual memory—seeing my father, with his neck wound about with a variegated yarn scarf that mother had knitted him, hauling in loads of yellow corn to be used as fuel! If you don't believe this last one, hunt up your histories and read of the strange doings of the 1880s. It is odd that I should recall these things and not remember the coming of my little baby brother, Joseph Edwin. He was born on January 19, 1885.

In March, Father left us to take his claim and build the sod house, returning sometime in April to take us to our new home. I remember clearly that ride in the covered wagon, the nights around the campfire, the loss of little Dora, our spotted terrier, and the big fight Tige, our mastiff, had with another dog. He came out victorious as always, but wearing the wounds of battle. A slivered ear and a gashed cheek meant nothing to his young life! Dear old Tige—what a friend he was to be in the days beyond us.

Sometimes as we jogged along, Elizabeth and I would sit on the seat with Father when Mother wished to lie back on the bed and rest. As I write, I wonder what she thought about at those times. Through the canvas stretched tightly over the hickory bows, the bright Kansas sunlight would filter in, creating a restful, mellow glow. She would hear the soft thud of the horse's hooves on the moist ground, the leathery squeak of the harness as they tugged up a rise, and the loose rattle of it as they went trotting down. I like to think she was going over again the things that Father had told her of the new home: that it was as fine a piece of land as there was in western Kansas, and that she would like the cozy sod house with its wide, deep windows for her geraniums. I would like to think that she was sharing some of the hope and anticipation that bubbled over from Father's songs as he entertained us children along the way. Father could sing, and oh, did he know the old ballads! He could sing many of the old English ones that were as long as your arm and had that peculiar dismal wail to them. Throughout all of my young life on the prairies, his songs were a joy to me.

About noon on the fourth day, we reached Jetmore, the county seat of Hodgeman County. Father bought provisions and talked longer than Mother thought he should to his new acquaintances about the previous trip. With only eighteen more miles to cover, Father thought that we'd be home in time to set up the stove, get the carpet down, and get the beds set up for a good night's sleep. We passed through Hodgeman Center, which not long before had fought Jetmore for the title of county seat. A schoolhouse, a store or two, and a few dwellings were left to tell the tale. Another few miles and we came to Laurel, which was to be our post office. The "office" was in Ben Cline's home. There was Lora, just my age, Cora, Elizabeth's age, and red-cheeked Ted. Father thought that we should stop and get acquainted with them, but Mother urged him on. In a mile or so, we came to the Glathearts, dear folks that we would come to know so well later on.

As we neared the crest of the hill beyond and approached the house from which we would view our own, we children were filled with excitement, crowding up against Father and Mother, that we might get the first glimpse of our new homeland.

Another moment and Father cried, "There she is!" He waved his arm proudly at the valley below. But something was wrong. In a few minutes, we were close enough to see what had happened. Heartsick and dismayed, we viewed the ruins of our home. Some thief had stolen the center ridgepole that had supported the roof, along with the windows and doors and the frames of each; every scrap of wood about the place was gone. Roofless, the house stood there like a skeleton. Mother was too stunned to even utter a word, and the tears began to flow.

"Let's go back to Linn County," Elizabeth said. Father began to berate in extra strong language against the man who had spoiled this dream of his. Sorely perplexed, his eyes gazed across the wide view of treeless land and rested upon a galloping rider coming from the right.

"It's Joe Cookun," he said.

Joe Cookun was a bachelor who had taken a claim and lived in a dugout half a mile northeast. He had helped Father build the soddy. He had been watching it for us and had meant to be there to help us unload, but just the day before he had discovered the tragedy and now hurried to tell us to drive on over to his house and make ourselves at home.

"Why, Dave and I can throw up another in no time," Joe said in an encouraging manner. He would allow no objections to his proposal and rode along at Father's side, uttering cusswords to the scoundrel who would do such a thing. Joe had tried to trace the tracks of the thief, but the trail was soon lost as it joined the road to Ravenna, another boomtown fifteen miles to the west.

Good old Joe gave us the sort of welcome that he would have given long-lost relatives. For many years afterward when we had an extra supply of provisions on hand, we would say with a flourish what he had said that day in his address of welcoming: "Why, I've got so much stuff to eat, it looks like Jones's Store at my house."

Joe's house was a combination of sod and dugout. A hole about seven feet square had been dug out from a bank and roofed over, the roof being slightly higher than the ground behind it. This was the bedroom. In front of this was a low sod room about ten feet square that primarily served as the kitchen. But as need arose, it resolved itself into a bathroom, dining room, or sitting room. My mother must have been grateful for the shelter, but how heartsick she must have been about the whole situation. On top of that, little Joe had a bad cold. I can definitely recall the shelves of canned goods, the table with its brown oilcloth, the cookstove in the corner, and the water shelf under one of the little four-paned windows.

It was evening when we arrived, and of course once Joe told her the whereabouts of everything, Mother began to prepare supper. Elizabeth tended the baby, and I was chosen to start the fire. And with what? Cow chips, of course! I think that was our first real experience of prairie life outside that of the ruined house. Somehow that job was given to me most of the time we were out there. It saved Mother from having to wash her hands so often while preparing the meals. The dried chips made a quick, hot fire but had to be replenished often. They left a cake of ashes practically the same size as the original chips, so the ashes had to be poked down through the front grating quite frequently to make room for more chips at the top. Soon we became accustomed to the use of them. Coal was expensive, and the distance far to haul. We had moved into a woodless country, and there was nothing to do but accept the fuel that the country offered.

If Father's spirits were ever down for more than a minute, my mother's good meals could always raise them back up. True to form, he and Joe began to talk of rebuilding on a nicer little knoll behind where the first house had stood. Joe planned to plow more sod while father drove six miles to Kalvesta the next morning to get more lumber.

BUILDING THE SODDY

Father was back by noon and took over the plowing. How he did enjoy it after fighting stumps and hidden roots to which he had been accustomed. Sod that had been trampled by thousands of buffalo and pranced over by just as many Indian ponies now bared itself to the plowshare of the pioneer.

Rich, black loam, matted and held together by the wiry roots of the short, curled buffalo grass rolled from the moldboard as one unbroken satin ribbon. With a spade the "ribbon" was cut into twenty-four-inch lengths. The house being already staked out, these lengths were carefully hauled and laid in a double row, end-to-end, grass side down, until the round was completed, thereby making the beginning of walls two feet thick. The next layer was laid, of course, overlapping the cracks in the first layer, and so on in a sort of brick laying fashion until the desired height was reached. Opening for doors and windows were planned and left.

While they were loading more sod, I amused myself by running barefoot around the walls until they began to leave the spaces for the windows, and then Father would put an end to my fun. As they went along, the partition walls were put in, tying them to the side walls by overlapping. The window frames were set in so the sod could be pressed securely against them—same with the door frames. When the walls reached about the height of seven feet, the low cable ends were built and the ridgepole was set in place, from end to end. A few rafters were placed from the pole to the walls on each side and it was then ready for the roof, pioneer style. Small willows the size of fishing rods were brought from the Pawnee River and laid across the rafters until the spaces were all covered. Then, a full layer of sod and another layer that would close the cracks were laid for the roof. It was not complete until a thick layer of magnesium clay brought from a nearby bank had been spread over it. The clay would dissolve with the first rain, forming a thick, smooth coating which shed the rain for quite some time before needing to be repaired.

Our new house faced the east. The kitchen was at the north end of the home, and the big sitting room was at the south and east. There were three bedrooms as well, all plastered. And for a ceiling, unbleached muslin was sewn together and stretched tightly in place. Straw was brought in to cover the grass floors of the sitting room and bedroom. The rag carpets were stretched over them and tacked down with shingle nails! The kitchen floor was just scraped clean of the grass, giving it a hard, solid floor. As I sat at the dinner table, I would always try to pull up a grass root with my toes.

And there was our house! But so alone it seemed. Not a tree, not a shrub, a post, or anything but that oblong box of sod. It was a little dot on a quarter section of land. But it was now our home and how glad we were to move in.

How well I remember the furniture! And it's amazing that so much of it could have been brought over in the covered wagon. For some reason, Mother put both beds in the sitting room—probably because there was little else to put in it! Well, the beds would have graced any room for that matter. They were made of maple and dressed in high-feather bedding, pretty old quilts, and pillow-shams done in "turkey-red" thread. The old walnut bureau was set in the corner. The two little top drawers were assigned to Elizabeth and me. There was also a little table, the small heating stove, some wooden chairs, and Mother's cherished Singer sewing machine. There was a cot in the bedroom and pegs in the walls for our clothes. Other than that, it was merely a place to set things.

The kitchen was the hub of our world; Mother was almost always there, kneading her great loaves of delicious bread, frying crisp doughnuts, making molasses cookies or baking those wonderful pies that were father's favorite food. The kitchen furnishings were made up of a cookstove, a drop-leaf table, a cook table, the water bench, the pierced tin-door safe, the cheery Seth Thomas clock on the wall, and the wooden, round-backed hickory chairs.

I think that the most satisfactory room to Mother was the "cyclone cave," which father had dug against the west wall of the kitchen with a little wooden door opening to the steps down in. Cyclones and rattlesnakes were Mother's greatest fear of the prairies. We didn't get to use it much to fool the cyclones, but what a wonderful place for the milk, butter, and cottage cheese! Canned fruit almost didn't exist, but there we kept the molasses keg, cucumber pickles, squashes, and the sauerkraut jar. Home-canned vegetables were an unknown art in those days, with perhaps the exception of tomatoes.

I don't know how long it took the men to finish the house. It seems to me that some of the other neighbors lent hands to the job, so it probably wasn't long, for I have heard of them tell of our moving in when the walls were still wet. Elizabeth and I came down with the whooping cough at that time as well!

"It's a wonder it didn't kill them both," I often heard them say.

With the family housed, father made a stable with the remnants of the house that had been demolished. He also made a little sod chicken coop. He stuck good water in the well near the house at thirty feet, and they walled it with rock from a nearby quarry.

NEIGHBORS ON THE PRAIRIE

And what about neighbors—should I say we had them? Clockwise, beginning with Joe Cookun, there was John Dickerson, who built his one-room house out of stone (the quarry being on his property). He was a bachelor, needing only one room. Beyond him lived Mr. and Mrs. Reed, who had no children. I remember them as very gracious and refined people. Mrs. Reed wore such dainty clothes, and Mr. Reed led the singing in our Sunday school, using a tuning fork to get the pitch. They were Presbyterians.

Back and a little to the right of them were the Moulds. They were from "York State." There was Mr. and Mrs. Mould and then Aunt Em, who was spacious and kind. Dan and Eva were almost, if not in, their teens, and Lizzie and Jesse were about my age. Jesse was my childhood boyfriend. If he ever had any sweets, he would always share them with me on the way to school. Once an uncle sent him some lovely bird pictures, several of which he laid on my desk during school hours. The teacher saw the lovely deed and promptly appropriated the pictures until we could have them out with us at recess! How rude some teachers are with their lack of understanding!

Next came the Woods; it was just the two of them in their soddy on the crest of the hill to the southeast of us. I liked to go up there to look at the pictures that Mrs. Wood had pasted on her kitchen walls. The Woods were from Ohio and the first to "pull out and leave this God-forsaken country," as they described it. After the Woods left, one of mine and Elizabeth's favorite pastimes was to go up and try to retrieve some of the pictures from the walls. The cardboard pictures came off very well, but the others were stuck to stay. The house soon fell into ruins after someone removed the timbers from it. Bought or stolen I cannot say, but our picture gallery was gone!

The Glathearts, from Pennsylvania, came next. They were members of the Brethren, or Dunkard Church, as we called them in those days. They were a lovely family. Their house was dug out of sod with a little frame attachment. They had a grown daughter named Delia and a teenaged son named Ed.

South of us were the Hamiltons, two girls who had lost their mother before coming out, the Hazelwoods with a few children, the Loves, the Dunns, the Lairds, and the Thorsons. Being some distance away, I do not recall being in any of their homes. They were all cattle farmers, and the young boys would frequently ride over in their fancy trappings to visit us (mainly Elizabeth). They were in another school district, so I didn't get acquainted with the families very much.

Swinging to the southwest were the Duncans, our nearest neighbors. They were from Kentucky. Tom Duncan was fat and jolly, and Lucy Duncan was even larger and more joyous and easy-going. They lived in a soddy, of course, and the children accumulated. There were George, Lizzie, Wilmot, Wood, Isaac, Rebecca, and Thelma—and they were still coming when we left. I have forgotten the names of the two younger ones.

Directly west of us were the Goodmans, also from Kentucky. They had two boys and a grown daughter. Soon after our arrival, the daughter died of tuberculosis; a little while later, the family left to head back to Kentucky. Many a time I would gather bouquets of wild flowers and take them to the lonely grave of their daughter. Its stone posts and barbed wire were silhouetted against our northern horizon.

To the northwest was the lively family of the Gierkies. They were Germans from Tennessee. They had a large family and worked "like Turks." The children were not in our school district, but we saw them occasionally and always when it was molasses time, for they had a sorghum mill. Life on the prairie without sorghum just wasn't considered possible.

To the north of the Pawnee lived jolly, bald-headed Ed Roberts, a bachelor. He could play the fiddle like wildfire, and the dances he put on at his house were amazing. People came from far and near when he sent out the word. Sweet cider and cookies were the usual refreshments, though oyster suppers were not infrequent. From where or how he obtained that sweet cider was always a mystery. He kept a little stock of groceries, and usually everyone went home with a sack of them after his dances.

Near the store lived the Hamms. Mr. Hamm was tall and wore sideburns, while Mrs. Hamm was stout, wore overalls, and wore her hair shingled! She had a little palsy and shook her head sideways when she talked. They had two nearly grown sons who, believe it or not, went by the names of Son and Darlin'! Mrs. Hamm was a really nice woman, but the pants and short hair were very hard for the settlers to take for a while! How sensible she was, though. It took ten yards of cloth to make any kind of dress in those days, and the wild winds would blow hair done in any fashion into a frizzled halo around the head two minutes after sticking it outdoors. They had come from Missouri and were one of the early families to leave.

Next were the Scotts. Mrs. Scott was always ailing, and I would go over to wash her dishes. She would usually give me a nickel or a piece of cake for the job. She also taught me how to make pan custard, and I went home thinking that I could tell my mother, "Why, I make the same thing, only I put it in a pie!" My sails went down; custard pie was my favorite!

There we were, many families living as simply as possible, thinking we could turn our piece of desert into a garden merely because it was given to us by the government, provided we would make certain improvements and lived thereon for five years. At that time, we could "prove up" and the homestead would really be ours. The land was rich, and with plenty of rainfall, the crops were abundant. Assured of rich land and hoping for sufficient rain, the boom was on. Everyone's hopes were high as they started to break their ground and farm. And we were not the last ones by any means. Every day we would see from two to half a dozen covered wagons heading westward.

One hundred miles of prairie lay between us and the Colorado line, and every acre of it seemed to be waiting for a homesteader. Since there were few fences, travelers took a bee line in the direction they were headed. The old Santa Fe Trail was only a few miles south of us; one day, Father took us over there and told us of the travelers who made their way across there a little more than thirty years before headed for the West in search for gold. It was not just one road, but as many as four or five, side by side; some of them had been deeply rutted, but all of them were grassed over. I've always been glad that he took the trouble to show us that.

Dodge City, the gathering place for the cowboys noted for its gambling and "shootin'," was only thirty miles southwest of us on the Arkansas River. Garden City was only a few miles farther on. So much for our location and environment.

We were scarcely settled in the little soddy before the neighbors began coming in. Mothers would bring their sewing or knitting and spend the day at our home. We children worried not in the least that Mother was expecting to feed everyone for dinner, but instead it was often four times that! Pies would quickly be shoved in the oven, soon to be followed by biscuits. Bacon was fried and dipped into the pickle keg and kraut barrel. If the hens were laying good eggs, we would have them. The grown folks and guests would eat first, and we would have to wait. That was always a trying time, but soon forgotten in another animated game of hide and seek, dare base, or drop the handkerchief.

All too soon, the man of the company would hitch up and shout, "It's time we best be heading home. Come on, everybody!" There were always more words exchanged, however, and it was usually a half-hour before the team got the signal to move on.

One of the very first and most welcome visitors was John Dickerson of the stone house. Here he came one evening, leading an old red cow named Bossie. He said that she wandered far away, and if we wanted to picket her out and water her, we could have her for the milk. Did we want the cow? I remember how good the gravy was for supper—and that next day we had custard pies! I hadn't missed the milk, for I did not like it, and I still don't!

Father wanted to buy her, but good-hearted John did not want to sell her. I suppose he had a reason and that was helping out a new settler. In a few weeks, he disappeared. We never heard of him afterward—except there was a rumor that he had been captured by a gang of horse thieves and hung near Dodge City. We all knew that if that was the truth, John was innocent. No one ever came for Bossie, and she ended up being ours.

THE SCHOOL DEBATE

It seems that the earlier settlers were the ones that had no families to speak of, but the later ones, like ourselves, came with the expectation of making a home with wives and children and building a community of interest. With that end in view, of course, a schoolhouse was the first necessity. Those who had children had been sending them to adjacent school districts, and that meant a long distance for many of the pupils. And in those days, school attendance was optional, which meant that many a youngster quit school very young. Of course, Father began to stir up the idea of having our own school as soon as he was fairly landed, which meant that he stirred up plenty of opposition too, because having a school meant taxation. And very soon, there was decided movement to squelch his idea. There had been many, however, who had long wanted the school and quickly rallied on father's side. And with father being a very good campaigner, the war was really on!

There was school land just a mile south of us. Father, with another neighbor, set out to find out how many claimholders were really in our district. They also went out to have Mrs. Glatheart, an older resident, call a meeting of these men and women on the school land for the purpose of voting bonds. By the time the day set for the meeting had arrived, the opposition had gained considerable support from even those who sent their children to other districts, since they would potentially be nearer to the school in the other district than the one in their own. So it appeared that a showdown fight was in the offing. Father and Mother were really early on the scene and he, of course, kept

THE CRAZY QUILT OF LIFE

close account of those arriving from both sides. It was now 9:30 in the morning, and the vote was to be taken at 10:00 a.m. The margin was so close in his favor that he was not comfortable and did wish that the Glathearts had brought their daughter Delia, who lived next to them and was proving up a claim of her own.

The bachelors opposing the school boasted that there would be no school in this district, for this was a cattle country and no place for "wimmen an' kids."

I could see father's gray eyes flash. With a quick word to Mr. Glatheart, he bounded into the wagon seat and took off in a jiffy, across the draw and up the long slope toward Delia's. Questions began to fly.

"He's going after my daughter, who is in favor of the bonds," Mr. Glatheart said calmly.

"Yes, but the voting is to be held in less than half an hour," said half a dozen at once.

"The meeting will be called to order at ten o'clock, friends—whether he is here or not. And I shall hold my watch here where you all can see," he replied as he held out the big silver timepiece.

The crowd was tense as they watched the horses reach the top of the hill and head down into a little depression that hid them from view.

"Now if Delia just won't think she has to change her dress," said Mrs. Glatheart to Mother.

"Ain't no way he can make it. Course not. He can't possibly get back in time," boasted one of the men. "Bet she ain't even home," he concluded with satisfaction.

"He can't?" shouted Joe Cookun. "Then what's that you see roundin' the knoll and rollin' down the hill? Partner, you can always come down a hill faster than you can go up it." Joe set up a whooping cheer that some joined, and others laughed. While there were very decided and strong opinions on the matter of the bonds, there was little bitterness.

Mr. Glatheart, as master of the ceremony, stood calmly with his big old watch in his hand. Only seven minutes left before the meeting would have to be called. He smiled a little as he watched the horses come on a dead run across the narrow valley and straight toward them.

As he took a look at the old watch, Joe cried out, "He can make it!"

And made it they did—with three minutes to spare—as he brought the lathered horse to a stop.

As Delia climbed down over the wagon wheel, my father laughed and said, "Well, Delia and I had quite a buggy ride!"

"And Delia changed her dress!" exclaimed her mother.

Mr. Glatheart called the meeting to order and talked earnestly of the necessity of not a schoolhouse in the district, but of the need for a building to have Sunday school and church when it could be had. The vote was taken after several had their say. The school won by one vote! What a relief.

Board members were selected, and the announcement was made that bids for the erection of the new building would be received on the following Monday. It was agreed that it should be built of lumber rather than sod, since it would be more durable and be of greater pride to the community. Father was selected as secretary of the board and instructed to write the minutes of the meeting, and it was adjourned.

What an interesting drama was played out there on the open prairies that day, and how proud I am of the part my mother and father played in it!

On the following Monday when Mr. Glatheart opened the bids, there were only two, and the work was given to Father. The first thing that he had to do was to work out a scheme whereby he could be a farmer and a carpenter at the same time now that he had the new job. He promptly sent for his youngest brother, William, who came on the next train to take a hand at farming or at the more simple art of carpentry as the case required.

How glad we were to see Uncle Bill. He was a jolly good fellow, and he joined right in with Father on the ballad singing and was good at his guitar. Of course that was his high rating as far as we children were concerned. Mother liked him too, for he was so good about doing his house chores when she was especially overloaded, which was most of the time.

That guitar was to us children something "just out of this world" (a slang phrase from the 1950s). After a long day at work, Uncle Bill and Father would bring out their chairs, tilt them back against the house, and the concert would begin. While the prairie is wonderful in the moonlight, I loved the starry nights best, for we would lie on our backs in the soft grassy yard. The music and the stars seemed to intermingle into all that this world had to offer. It was a sort of perfection.

It was a beautiful summer in Pleasant Valley. The crops were wonderful, the schoolhouse progressed, and we were getting further and further along with our acquaintances with the neighbors. By driving to Dodge City, twelve miles farther than Jetmore, Father found that he could save in the cost of material—and so he went there for most of it. Each time he would bring us a little treat of some kind, and I especially remember the bag of delicious peaches, perhaps half a dozen, and in the bottom of the sack a few plums. What a feast in a fruitless country!

On one trip he took the family, starting by daylight and pulling in home long after dark. It's strange that among all of the interesting things that there must have been to see there, I remember only the sight of the "Old Soldiers' Home" as we passed it on our return home. And the "Boys in Blue" were not so old, either; the Civil War was only twenty years behind us. Some were on cots in the yard, others were moving about on crutches, and a number were being wheeled about in wheelchairs by nurses in white uniforms. Elizabeth decided then and there that she intended to be a nurse as soon as she was old enough. I remember feeling glad that Father had not been old enough to enlist; he was thirteen when the war was declared.

The schoolhouse was finished in time for the opening of the six-month term. A well had been dug, two little toilets far to the back had been set up, and the winter's coal was in the basement. Mr. Shawn was chosen as teacher, and all was ready for the beginnings of my education. And furthermore, the teacher was going to board and room at my house! This meant, of course, that we would have cakes, pies, and doughnuts about every day. I know I felt a little superior that the teacher had chosen to stay with us.

I, of course, was under school age but was allowed to go and play or work as I chose. I chose most of the time to play, making a playhouse on the windowsill next to my desk. Father had bought my First Reader and slate; what I learned that first year enabled me to go into the Second Reader class the next year. I'm sure it was not because of any special aptitude of mine, but merely because it was handier for the teacher.

AN EARLY AMERICAN CLASSROOM

There was a row of five double seats on each side of the room, enough for twenty pupils. In the middle of the room sat the big pot-bellied stove, around which we hovered to warm our fingers on frosty mornings if we managed to get there a few minutes before "books took up." Up front was the teacher's table, of course. No polished apples ever found their way to the desk, however, because they were non-existent except at Christmas. We did, however, share our molasses taffy and popcorn balls with him.

Going back to the furnishings of the room, it's about all said except for the blackboard, erasers, and chalk. The border of the blackboard was painted about a yard in depth all the way around, and there was a rail nailed at the bottom to hold the chalk and erasers.

Some agent selling school supplies convinced the board that we needed not only an encyclopedia, but large wall maps as well, made in the form of a book. Each page was a country, and when closed, the back of it was a blackboard! All the maps were in beautiful color; how I loved that map book! I don't know when I went in to the "gogerfy class," but when I did, I know that I already knew something about geography, for I couldn't stay away from those beautiful colored panels showing us the great oceans and the many countries with their strange sounding names. The names of the capes and the bays intrigued me—so much so that I would name the new calves after them! I named one of the last ones Cape Farewell Lizzie Duncan. I also made a great game called "finding places" that we played by naming the first letter of a cape or country and then cruising around with our fingers on the map until we found it, either in a small area or just naming the word and then having the others search the entire page guided by someone using the hot-and-cold method.

It is no wonder that even now *National Geographic,* with its fine maps, delightfully descriptive articles, and worldwide views in full color, is my most loved magazine because I have always been intrigued by maps and the like.

The schoolhouse was in truth the community center. Political meetings were held, a debating society was organized, there were spelling matches and the singing school met and practiced there as well. It was our church too. A Sunday school was immediately organized after the building was constructed. Mr. Allen, an Episcopalian not long since from England, was elected superintendent. He was a widower, kind and very religious, with red hair and a redder face.

On the first Sunday, he proposed that beginning with the following Sunday, we should each memorize a verse beginning with A and then continue that process throughout the alphabet. I've been grateful for his plan many times, for it opened the Bible to me—and I know it did for others. To me, it was a fine game leafing through mother's big Bible. It was almost too big to fit on my little lap. I would sit on the floor, flipping the pages and looking for the right verse while I read many, many more. Many gems I placed in my "storehouse" then, and today they are as bright as when I stored them. Going over them on a sleepless night, I often wonder at the good selections I made; I usually was looking for the shortest verse possible—no matter what the content. For example: *Can the Ethiopian change his skin or the leopard change his spots?* And I didn't even play fair on that one, for it was only half of the verse!

Two of the verses I will leave with you are: "A good name is rather to be chosen than great riches, and loving favor rather than silver and gold." Also, "Favor is deceitful, beauty is vain, but a woman who feareth (loveth) the Lord shall be praised." These are from Proverbs, the book with enough wisdom in it to cure all of the world's ailments if it were applied.

Occasionally we had church services led by ministers of the Brethren denomination, invited by the Glathearts, who were devout members that constantly observed all its rules. Mrs. Glatheart always wore the little bobbinet cap in the house, and when going out, she wore the little stiff black bonnet over it.

So the first sermon that I ever heard was preached by Brother Keller. He was a very small man, and his wife was tinier. They roomed with the Glathearts, but all homes were open to them. It was a great day for me when they had dinner and supper at our house. So often when I look at the little glass lamp on my bedside table, now electrified, I recall lighting it for him when he was trying to read in the twilight. I would say, "You'll strain your eyes." My heart glowed when he smiled and patted my head.

It was in that two weeks of meetings that I had, I suppose, my first religious impulse. Among the crowd was a man who was little thought of in the community; as the preacher talked of Christ's love, I felt a wave of pity for him and decided that I should love him too since Christ did! Several young people joined the church, including sister Elizabeth. I would have too, but Father said I was too young. Our folks were Baptist; they, like most of the other older folk, clung to the original faiths. There was some objection to the girls becoming members since they would be obliged to wear those caps and bonnets. Elizabeth was strong in her convictions, however, and bonnet or no bonnet, she was going to be a Christian. The church furnished the bonnets, for they were to be made after an exact pattern, and they came in a very short time. It was a brown silk, if you please, lined with pink silk and with it several of the net caps. Only a few days would she wear the caps and the bonnet was soon laid aside also. Whether she felt that she had "fallen from grace," I don't know, but I doubt it. She had a rather logical mind.

When we moved to Jetmore, she, Mother, and I united with the Congregational church. I can see her now, singing in the choir, wearing a little brown velvet toque which was the hat of the day.

CHRISTMASTIME

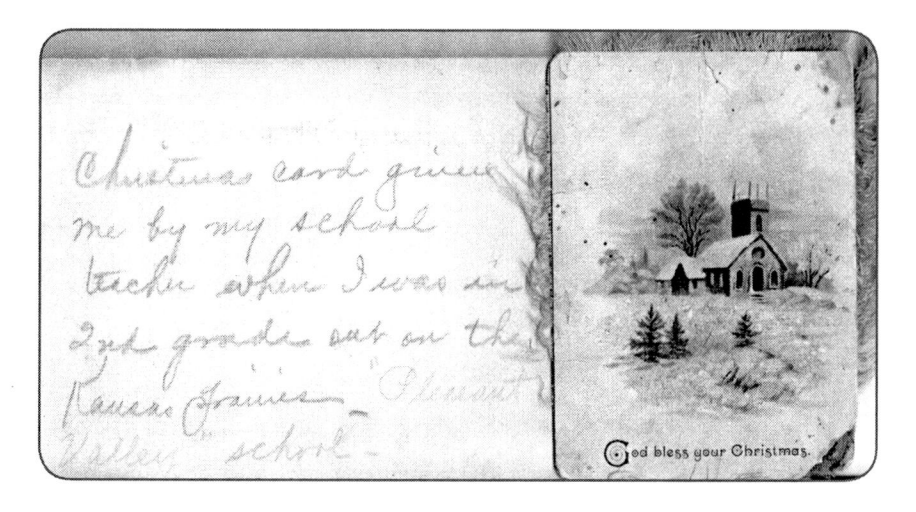

As a child, of course, the highlight of the school and community activities was that wonderful night of Christmas Eve. Celebrating Christmas back then was much different than it is today; the tree was especially different. With no evergreen trees nearer than the Rocky Mountains some 300 miles away or more (shipping Christmas trees then was a thing undreamed of), something unusual had to be done to produce that tree.

All of the settlers were from the eastern states where to have a cedar or pine meant only to go to the woods and haul one in to be made the center of the family festivities. Everyone knew that without a tree it couldn't be Christmas! Father met the problem with his unusual optimistic solution that required no precedent.

"Why," he said to the committee, "we can have a tree that will outshine anybody's Christmas tree. I saw a pretty little hackberry over on the Pawnee River the other day—one with lots of branches. Tom and I can bring that over and fasten it on a box, the women can decorate it with sacks of candy and strings of popcorn, and then we will hang on the presents. And yes, we can even buy a bushel of apples and tie one at the end of every twig. Who will say that we do not have a Christmas tree?"

To him, the idea was complete. But someone, likely a woman, thought it would add so much to its beauty to wrap every limb with strips of tissue paper of all colors! And all agreed.

The month before that great day, the teachers found themselves quite busy selecting songs and recitations and listening to rehearsals as soon as the lines were memorized. The several Christmases that were in that time of my life have been merged into one memory—except for my two speeches. The first of which starts out with:

> *I stepped upon the stage*
> *My heart went pit-a-pat*
> *And all the people said*
> *"Whose little girl is that?"*

Another time that stands out sharply was when I was about eight and recited "Two Little Stockings," which told of a little girl who hung up an extra stocking for a poor little girl with a note telling Santa to put it all in Carla's bag if he didn't have enough for both. Of course Santa had enough, with some extras for the main girl because she had thought of the poor.

The day, which seemed like it would never come, showed up one cold morning when the ground was covered with a deep, crusty snow. Father had lifted the box from the wagon and placed it on runners that he had just finished. Away he and Tom went for the tree, not expecting to be back until noon. There was little for me to do except watch Mother put the finishing touches on my new dress and "practice my piece," which I could already say in a sing-song manner.

Father came back at noon saying the tree was up. It was a beauty, and he said he would take Elizabeth back with him to help the others who were coming to decorate it and put the presents on. Father pulled a box out from under the bed, and I hadn't known it was there! Christmas presents were ready to hang, but not a peep was I allowed.

For Christmas, Mother had curled my bangs with tin curlers that she had made by cutting narrow strips from a tin can and wrapping them with paper. She would roll up a lock and bend the ends over the roll until it was held in place. The back of my hair was in two braids, not very long, fine as silk almost, and about the color of a lemon! I had little color to my skin, and my lips were too thick—at least that's what I thought. It was the kind of worry known only to my childish mind.

Suppertime was near, and Father and sister had arrived. He hurried to do the chores, and she hurried to wash up and dress little Joe while I helped set up the table. I was too excited to eat much. In fact, we all hurried through supper. Father had the key and wanted to get to the tree early to light it up before anyone came.

As we approached the presents, my face was shining. The moment came, and I opened up a new dress. What a thrill! It was a marine blue worsted with raised figures of a deeper hue and a blue ribbon sash with ribbons to match for my hair. It was the prettiest dress I had ever seen, and there was no telling how many pounds of butter or dozens of eggs had been traded for the fabric and ribbon to make such a piece of clothing.

I got a hood and mitten to match as well! My hood was made using shell stitching, and it had a full ruffle around my face. When I slipped it on and looked in the mirror, I thought that my yellow bangs and blue hook looked pretty together—and that I wasn't so bad looking after all.

When I had preened a little and put on a few airs, Mr. Funston, the teacher who sat waiting for us to get ready, said, "When I come back from my vacation at Jetmore, I'm going to bring you a present." He wouldn't tell me what, but when he did, he revealed that it was a little book called *Fine Feathers Don't Make Fine Birds*. I put a little idea into his head, and he put a big one into mine. I think it must have been so; for as far back as I can remember, clothes to me have meant merely something that must be worn.

We all climbed into the sled. Father, Mother, and Joe in the spring seat, Mr. Funston on a little stool just back of them, and Elizabeth and I on comforts that had been spread over hay. It was a very cold night, and the snow creaked under the sled runners as Sam and Mart swung into a fast trot, the air stinging our faces red.

As we drew up to the schoolhouse, Father gave me the key and said, "Here, you get to unlock and get the first peeps since you didn't get to help decorate."

I was out of that sled and to the door like a streak. Unlocking it, I experienced sensations unlike any Christmas before or since. First there was the sheltering warmth and in the darkness the low fire flickering through the draft openings in the big stove, the combination of odors of rare and delicious sweets like oranges, apples, and popcorn. And then, as my eyes became accustomed to the darkness, there at the front in the right-hand corner was the great tree reaching to the ceiling. When the folks came in, I hadn't moved a step. I felt that I had been planted and taken root in a kind of fairyland.

Removing our wraps, we stood around the stove while Father lit the sputtering bracket lamps on the wall. We were told to not go near the tree but to sit down. So, as you may have guessed, we sat in the seats nearest to the tree, exclaiming over what we were beholding: a tree of many colors, loaded with an assortment of gifts such as you could not imagine. There was no tinsel, no lights, but only the strings of popcorn woven in and out among the gifts that were brought to display, not wrapped in gay papers and tied with gayer ribbons and deposits at the foot of the tree in piles.

No, indeed, the gifts were to be seen and appreciated by all. There were folds of dress goods, new shirts, overalls, socks, and caps. Square silk mufflers for the men, fascinators and hoods for the women and girls, handkerchiefs galore hanging from one corner, bright hair ribbons dangling from a tender twig, and mingled through all of this wearing apparel were the net sacks of candy and the precious orange suspended. Over all the tree swung bright red apples, which made our mouths water; oranges and apples were to be had only at Christmas. Near the base of the tree a new saddle was thrown over a heavier limb with a new bridle nearby. A handmade bootjack leaning up against a pair of heavy boots stood at the base of the tree.

Yes, there were a few toys like inexpensive dolls and thin picture books. I couldn't take my eyes off of a little yellow-haired doll up near the top, and I tried to make believe that some other girl's name was pinned on her. But if she by the slightest chance should be mine, her name would be Fairy.

The house was being filled rapidly, and I was still trying to locate "the little round thing" when the teacher rapped for order and the program began with a song by the school. Then away we went with song and recitations with some on the theme of Christmas but most of them not. "Curfew Must Not Ring Tonight" and "Kentucky Belle" were favorites that just had to be given, no matter what the program. The songs were usually patriotic. There were no Christmas carols known by us, much less sang. The nearest thing to it was the last item in the program. Just before Santa Claus leaped in through the side window, Lizzie and I sang:

> *Merry Christmas bells are ringing*
> *Joyfully they sound*
> *Santa Claus is coming o'er the frozen ground*
> *See him now approaching, loaded down with toys*
> *Bringing many good gifts for the girls and boys*
> *Ring the merry bells, ring the merry bells*
> *Ring, ring the merry Christmas bells!*

Then, as you can imagine, the house was in a riot of welcome to the old man with rope whiskers who told the usual story of being stuck in a snowdrift, which made him late getting there, and he'd have to hurry on. With that, he picked an apple from the tree, tossed it to someone, told them to distribute the gifts, and out the window he popped.

Santa's deputy and carriers soon stripped the tree, and all was confusion and fun. As the man reached for the fair-haired doll, I held my breath. And then, as he held her out to me, I thought that the world was mine. I also got a little squawking parrot made out of fragile papier-mâché. And what do you suppose the little round thing was? A glass hobnail saltshaker! That didn't go over very big then, but it is a treasure now; it sits on my dressing table. It is a lovely holder for corsage pins.

I remember the ride home that night for two things: the nearness of the stars as they twinkled down at us and the tragedy that happened to my parrot. She gave her last squawk when I accidentally sat down upon her as I moved to a more comfortable position for myself and Fairy. No happier girls went to bed that Christmas Eve than I, holding my new doll in my arms and being very thankful that I had not forgotten "my piece."

FAMILY LIFE

Lida, Father, Bill, Joe, Minnie Elizabeth, and Mother

The first few years in the soddy were friendly years. Crops were good, and the settlers began improving their claims, mainly by fencing and increasing their herds. Houses were being enlarged for growing families as well. Father laid out an orchard, planted his locust grove, and from the nearby stone quarry, drilled and hauled enough stone posts to fence his quarter section. Elizabeth suggested that "Locust Grove" would be a nice name for our place, and that's what we called it.

Western Kansas was really on the boom. More covered wagons were trekking west beyond us, and more residences and business houses were being built in the little towns that had sprung up not far from us. "It's a great country," was the universal verdict, and all the settlers looked forward to the time when frame houses would replace the sod ones.

There was enough to do around the house that we were all kept fairly busy; Mother worked too hard though, with no conveniences except her sewing machine to make her work easier. There were big washings, ironings, and baking days. On those, she would make half-dozen great loaves of bread, several pies, and a crock of doughnuts or cookies for lunches for us and the teacher (his lunches were always separate though, apart from the regular meals).

All of our clothing she made, of course, besides knitting mittens, stockings, hoods, etc. She crocheted lace for all of our underwear, which she made from flour sacks. And at night she sewed carpet rags with inch-wide strips of worn-out garments, tacking the ends together, and then wound them into large balls. When she had so many pounds, she would take them to a neighbor who wove them into a carpet for us. Her hands were never idle, it seemed, for she kept the little soddy spotless.

Like every child on the farm, I early learned to help with the housework and the outside chores as well. I much preferred the outside work and going along with Father in the wagon whenever he would permit me. I milked a cow, fed the horses, and could harness them and lead them to water. I carried water from the well, brought in the fuel, fed it to the stove, dried the dishes, set the table, and forever was sweeping the kitchen and doorway much to my disgust.

I liked to go with Father and Elizabeth to help gather the winter's fuel. To the west was a high, open range, upon which no one had filed, and where small herds were often taken to graze (which afforded us an excellent source of supply). Father would put on the double sideboards, throw some gunnysacks on the wagon, call to us to climb in beside him on the spring seat, and away we would go. My face was hidden in my pink sun bonnet, which was discarded as soon as we were well out of sight of the house!

Mother would say, "I don't want you to get as black as Indians," but how I did hate that scratchy old bonnet against my ears. We would find plenty of chips, crisp and dry, which we girls and little Joe would put into piles. Father would follow up with the sacks and throw the sacks into the wagon. Occasionally in our search, we would run across a pair of buffalo horns, or perhaps just one, which we would carry home as a prize. Once Father found a rusted revolver gun, of which the wooden part of the handle had long since rotted away.

"Now that could tell us a story if it could talk," said Father. And all the way home, we conjured up tales about how it came to be there. I think that Joe still has it. I loved those days; they meant much more to me than the mere gathering of fuel. I felt as wild and free as the wind as I ran from place to place. I would gather the prairie flowers as much as picking up the chips!

Over a part of this area was a prairie dog town, covering several acres. They are little animals related to the groundhog, though very much smaller, and perhaps for protection, they like to be sociable and dig their holes very near to each other. They were lively little creatures and would not let us get too near to them; if they saw us coming, they would scamper to their holes and sit up on their hind legs on the mound of dirt they had just dug out and bark at us until we would just get too near. Then they would flip and be gone into their holes instantly.

Settlers considered it a calamity when a prairie dog town was started on their claim; not only did the mounds hinder cultivation, but the little dogs would eat the crop! Also, it was an undesirable place for grazing cattle. The little animals left small amounts of grass to graze upon, and their holes were a hazard as well; the cattle would often step into a hole when running and sprain a leg. However, the prairie dog towns always fascinated me—not only because of the impudence of the little dogs—little prairie owls also inhabited the holes and would disappear almost as quickly.

Jackrabbits, cottontails, tiny striped ground squirrels, and meadowlarks all made the prairie an enchanted place for me. Father was such an observer that he pointed out many things of interest to us. For instance, how the sunflowers, which glorified the prairies, always turned their faces to the sun and how much their seed meant to the birds in the winter. He showed us the tiny seeds of the buffalo grass, which were hidden beneath the grass on wiry, curly little stems.

You would be interested to know how we stored the chips for winter. First we made a large circle of the chips with the edges close together. Then we placed another layer upon that, overlapping the edges, and so on until it must have been three feet high. Then, into this enclosure, we would throw the chips, heaping them up in the center to a peak. Father would begin at the edge and place them around and around, always overlapping in a shingle-fashion until he reached the top. Then it would be capped over with some extra large ones. It was surprising how this shed the water and kept the interior dry. In the summer, the ones soaked from the winter weather would be dry again and be used for fuel.

Another delight of autumn days would be helping Father "head and strip" the sugar cane, making it ready for the sorghum mill. After he had cut off the glossy, ripe heads of grain, I would put them into piles, which made it easier to sack them. While the stalk was still standing, he would strip off the leaves, then cut the stalks and lay them into neat piles, ready to be laid into the wagon the next day and taken to the mill. This had to be done before frost to ensure good molasses. Sorghum molasses was a very important food item in the West in those days; it was our mainstay for sweets. Cookies and cakes, besides the molasses itself, constituted a large part of our diet. It was fun to ride over to the mill and have a big play with the Gierkie girls and watch the cane be fed into the mill. The juice would run out one side and the limp, dry stalks on the other as the old horse hitched to one end of the long pole, tramped round and round, turning the mill. We did not stay until all of it was ground or to see it boiled but would return in a few days for our wooden keg of rich, thick molasses.

That molasses! So often when we would return from school during the winter, Mother would have the large old iron stone platter heaped with taffy twists, which were thick with peanuts, raised and roasted by her. Or perhaps it would be piled high with popcorn balls, waxy with the golden sweet. Some of you must cherish that platter and hand it down, for it was given to her by her mother.

THE CRAZY QUILT OF LIFE

On another autumn day, we had the surprise of our lives when we came home from school to meet our new baby brother. William John was named after two of Father's brothers. They couldn't say that the doctor had brought him in his handbag; there had been no doctor. Mrs. Glatheart had to "bring him." Very early that morning, Father had awakened us, saying he was going to take us over to Duncan's for breakfast before we would go to school with their children. I was all excitement because this was something new. I dressed quick as a cat, and Elizabeth kept pace with me. So we were in the wagon by the time Father had the horses hitched to it.

We hurried over the short distance, and Father called out to the Duncans. Mrs. Duncan was already up and seemed to understand; she gave a few hurried directions about the breakfast and the school lunch. Snatching her bonnet, she was up in the spring seat in a jiffy, despite her heavy weight. And away they went back home. In the slang of today, 1951, I was completely flabbergasted! No one seemed ready to enlighten me about such queer goings on. I soon forgot the mystery in the fun all of us were having, as one-by-one, the youngsters began tumbling out of bed, rubbing their eyes, and without question thought it was a lark that we had come over for breakfast.

Mr. Duncan soon came in from the barn for his own breakfast. He told us to eat without so much gabbing, fix our lunches, and get ready for school. Often through the day, I would puzzle my small brain about the morning's strange procedure. So I lost no time getting home when school was out. The teacher went home with Ed Glatheart. The mystery was responsible of course for the memory of that beautiful October day, the nineteenth. The sky was hazy and the usual wind wasn't blowing. It was cool and refreshing after the heat of the summer. On that kind of October day, I still connect with the little baby brother.

As Joe grew older, he and I became the cowboys on the place. When milking time was over, we would turn the cattle out to pasture. And when evening came, we would round them up and drive them into the corral to be milked. I can see him now with his little old towhead, pushing against Reddy's flank, and a double stream of milk making music as it hit the pail below. If she moved, he would say, "Aww, Reddy!" Joe would beat me at the business, all right. Reddy was his cow. He fed her and petted her, and she followed him all over the place.

One evening I heard Joe shout, "Look at me!" He was stiff-legged, holding onto Reddy's tail and letting her pull him up to the corral. When I saw that she stood for it, I too grabbed a tail, which just happened to be of the herd bull. And no, he didn't fight. He just pulled me right on in. But when we told Father what we had done, he laughed and said that I had better hitch onto a cow next time. The soles of our shoes were as slick as sled runners—and the grass so thick and short—that we had a grand time sliding up that long and low hill up to the corral.

Joe and I always found something interesting to do with our imagination supplying the larger part of it. From the hill beyond the big draw, some distance from the house, there bubbled in the spring a little spring. So small, in fact, that with mud and stone, we could dam it, making us a toy lake over which we would sail a leaf boat. Then we would dock our leaf boats and do some imaginary fishing. By the next day, the dam would be broken, of course, and the little stream would wait for another one of our little projects. The great and destructive Johnstown Flood supplied us with an excellent idea. We built a nest of little mud houses, built the dam as large as we could. Then one of us ran down the hill, yelling at the top of our voice, "Flee to the hills for your lives! Thousands of people are in danger of drowning!" These were the words of the writers at Johnstown. The other would smash the dam and away would go the mud houses.

In that area, there were very large anthills, and we often would sit by them and watch the large ants as they would bring to the surface tiny pebbles that they excavated from their deep underground home, making more room for the growing colony. As long as we did not disturb them, they paid no attention to us. I particularly enjoyed running my fingers through the coarse, multicolored pieces of gravel around the outside edge of the hills. Looking closely at a handful one day, to my amazement I found an Indian bead. We began searching and found a few others. I was so excited as we ran home to tell the tale, for we knew that there was an Indian buried under the ant hill. Mother was as wonderstruck as we were; when Father came home, he was surprised and interested too.

When I said that we should dig him up to get the beads, Father said, "Oh no, we'll just let the old Indian rest in peace."

And all of my attempts at persuasion couldn't move him. The next time that Mel Torson came over, my favorite cowboy, I showed him my trophies, thinking he might be interested in the diggings.

He said, "No. I don't want to go down and meet that old Indian. I would rather just buy you some beads."

So what's left of that old Indian must still lie under that anthill.

But one day Mel brought the cutest little Indian bead purse for me. He said, "I found it in Dodge City the other day."

Happy? I should say I was. And I probably looked at it so much that I wore it out! However, its memory stayed with me; not long ago, I saw some like it among some antiques and in another moment it was mine. It is now in the bookcase with my other Indian relics, waiting for you to see.

INDEPENDENCE DAY

The one big event of the year besides Christmas was the Fourth of July celebration at Jetmore. It seemed that the county's whole population poured into the county seat.

We always went early to be in time for the parade, which was headed by the drum and fife corps. And next marched the "Boys in Blue," quite a large company, and then the Grand Army of the Republic. The little children followed, carrying flags and singing the "Battle Hymn of the Republic." Following that would be men and women on horseback, as many as could be induced to enter.

Father would hurriedly unhitch the horses and saddle Old Sam for Elizabeth while she slipped on her long riding skirt of black cambric over her dress while riding her side saddle, her most prized possession. When she was off to join the others in the parade, Father would take the spring seat off the wagon, set it under mulberry tree in the courthouse lawn, and tell Mother to have a seat. He would carry the baskets of dinner over. He left Mother to watch the baskets and the children while he set forth to find neighbors and friends. We would not see him again until it was time to eat. He usually came back with some hungry soul to eat with us.

In the meantime, the children immediately began cramming mulberries, resulting in stained fingers that were much to Mother's disgust. I took Joe to Jimmy Grant's store across the street to get some candy to mix with the berries. Jimmy, seeing our stained hands, offered to perform magic to chase away the stains. He lit a slow burning sulfur match and told us to cup our hands over it for a second, which we did, but not holding our hands too close. And to our astonishment, when we opened our hands, the stains were gone! It was surely magic. He smiled and gave us some sacks to put some berries in to take home. Now the popping matches of today won't do it; don't try it, or you will get burned.

I was rich that day, for I had a quarter that I had earned by picking bugs from our potato plants. And because Joe had a similar amount, we went on a spending spree of candy, lemonade, and our first ice cream. I spent my last nickel on large, thin, chewing gum hearts with pictures of flowers pasted in the middle. The gum was no more than sweetened paraffin, but how good! And I chewed until my jaw ached. Joe spent his last money on firecrackers.

Soon after noon, the games started. There was the potato race, the fat man's race, the sack race, the egg race, and more that I can't recall. Then the speaker came. Mother wasn't interested and always wanted to start home by that time. But not so with Father. He would stay "until the last dog was hung," Mother would say. At last everybody was tired. We piled into the wagon and set out for home, hoping to reach it before dark. From my recollection, that was never accomplished. I can still feel myself being pulled out of the hay, so sleepy I could scarcely stand. As I stumbled toward the house in the dark, I would beg to go to bed with my clothes on!

Late homing didn't bother Father; he was very interested in politics and never missed an opportunity to attend political rallies or to talk politics with anyone who would listen. Whenever a speaker of note was to be at Jetmore, he would go no matter what. Once he asked me to go with him to listen to Congressman Jerry Simpson from the "Big Seventh District," of which our county was a part of.

Jerry was a member of the Populist Party, which was a reform party made up mostly of Democrats and others who would join them to fight the trusts, regulation of railroads, and other injustices placed upon the common man by the wealthy, privileged classes.

I was nine or ten when Father and I drove those eighteen miles to hear the speech. I remember listening intently. Some of the speech went over my head, of course, but it was so punctuated with jokes and ridicule that I thoroughly enjoyed it. Jerry Simpson played a part in setting the course of our family running in a different direction. A few years later, he appointed Father to a job at the state hospital at Osawatomie!

THE STORIES OF SAM AND MART

I think that no story of our life on the claim would be complete without the part that Sam and Mart (the horses) played in it. Though often they did play havoc! Sam was a treasure; large, black, and gentle as a dog, he was the pet of the family. Sam would let us children climb all over him and as many could ride him as could hold on! Now it's a very different story about Mart. He was smaller than Sam, a dun (light tan), and treacherous to the point that Father wouldn't even ride him. He would run away at the drop of a hat. Though Mart had seen a thousand tumbleweeds roll across the prairies, if one happened to roll directly in front of him, with a loud snort he would lunge to one side, plunge forward, and a runaway was on. Sam didn't want to run, but like many human beings when they get into fast company, they just go along. All that Father could do was to try to keep them going in a circle or head them, if possible, to a plowed field where the traveling was tougher and they would eventually tire out and stop.

I have heard Father tell this story so often that it is so impressed on my mind. I am going to quote him. He read it after I had written it out for an earlier story and approved it:

> I had as good a little team as ever hauled a load. They'd out pull any team of their size in the country. But Mart was a fool! Got scared at his shadow and would run like mad no matter what he was hitched to. One afternoon I took the children with me to gather a few chips that I had piled up in the pasture and had only loose boards on the

running gears where I had been hauling stone posts. I was then herding some cattle for a neighbor and an old white ox that was dissatisfied since his mate had died began to wander away from the herd. So handing the lines to Elizabeth, I started off to circle around him and drive him back. I had gone but a few hundred yards when I heard a clatter, and I looked around just in time to see the last board fly off the wagon. Anne and the baby already spilled and Elizabeth, sitting on the coupling pole, tried to hold those runaway horses! I ran back toward them, shouting at the top of my voice. The horses knew what I was trying to and circled away from me.

"Let 'em go, let 'em go!" I shouted, but she held on. They headed for a gulley, and I felt sure that she would be killed. That time I sure would have shot that team dead if I could have got near them, but down into that gulley they went and when they came out the back wheels had turned over, twisting the hickory coupling pole, and still there was Elizabeth's red hood bobbing up and down, sticking to those horses like a leech. Presently the back wheels came off, which they would of course, being run backwards. And when that occurred, she was able to turn their course directly toward the newly plowed wheat field. I ran as fast I could and prayed that she would be spared from those flying wheels. They didn't run far after they hit that loose ground, for the back axle, of course, plowed right into it. By the time that I got up to them, that girl had unhitched those horses and was leading them toward home. I said "Elizabeth, why in the world didn't you jump and let those wild beasts go?" And she replied, "Why my sakes, that's what Hezzy Bacon did and you know that the whole neighborhood laughed at him for being such a coward." When we arrived home, Mother said her usual phrase, "Those horses will be the death of some of this family, yet!"

That story was all the fault of Mart. The only bad thing that Sam ever did, and who could blame him on that hot and windy day, was to dump me into the middle of a large buffalo wallow (which was still full of water from recent rain). I rode him bareback out after some cattle one day; he sniffed the water and made for it so that he could roll around and cool off. He pulled for the middle of the pond, where the water was deepest, started to lie down, and all of my kicking and yelling was of no avail when a bath was in prospect. The only thing left for me to do was to get myself up as he let himself down. Standing on his back, I bent my knees and jumped the farthest that I ever jumped, which was still two feet from the shore. I might as well have gone down with Old Sam, for with the splash I made I couldn't have been any wetter. Sam walked out and stood for me to climb on his back, but he was so slick I couldn't make it up. So taking the bridle, I led him on home, where I was laughed at a plenty.

The ponds scattered over the prairies were made by the buffalo when they would find a little water in a depression, crowd into it, tramping and wallowing, making it larger and deeper (not usually over three feet deep in the middle). Now that the buffalo were gone, they were all grassed over but still held water. These ponds were a delight to the stock as well as to wild creatures. Of course, in real dry weather, they soon went bare by the means of evaporation.

A LAND OF EXTREMES

As I look back upon the years we spent out there on the prairies, it seems that it was a land of extremes. There were mainly just two things: the flat land with its distant horizons and the pale bluish sky like a huge bowl turned down over it. The sun could shine the brightest, the wind could blow the hottest, the ground could get the driest, the snow could drift the highest, and the storm clouds got the blackest, creating the most terrific lightning and thunder in the world.

The blizzards and drifting snow! We awoke one morning with the wind howling like a pack of wolves; the world grew whiter every minute as the snow piled deeper and deeper against the south windows of the house. Some of the snow sifted in between the loose sashes. I'm sure my first words are what yours would have been if you had been there sitting up in bed and peering up at the mad and whirling snow.

"Do we have to go to school today?" I asked.

"I should say not," Father answered.

I scooted back under the cover while he built a good, warm fire to dress by.

That day and others like it were like stolen holidays. There was something cozy about being shut in—a comforting sense of protection against the wild, cold cruelty out of doors. To pass the time, Father and Mother played checkers using white and yellow corn for the men and the underside of the dough board marked off as a checkerboard. For us kids, it was tic-tac-toe, hide the thimble, and of all things, playing school. We included the grownups in this game, allowing them to continue playing checkers. We did this to show off our superior learning. Elizabeth would ask them to name the bones of the body or trace the circulation of the blood; my questions were to name the countries and capitals of Europe or all of the states in our country and their capitals. Father would sing out "Maine, Maine, Augusta on the Kennebeck River," and continue throughout the New England states and then he would say, "Oh, I give up!" When he went to school in a log schoolhouse in Indiana, they really had the states and capitals set to the music of "Go tell Aunt Rhody her old gray goose is dead." They could beat us every time in arithmetic; when it came to spelling, Father could out-spell anybody (providing they stuck to *McGuffey's Speller*).

In the afternoon of the snowy day, we calmed down considerably. Elizabeth had learned to crochet and was busy with lamp mats, chair tidies, and picture throws (now if you don't know what all these things are, ask your grandmother). I would piece on my nine-patch quilt or work on memorizing a poem to recite on some special day. If the supply of lamplighters was low, I would make a dozen or so, for that was one of my special jobs. How? Just by rolling a long, narrow strip of paper into a hollow tube and bending down the end. It would stay rolled, and they made fine substitutes for matches. We never thought of striking an extra match if there was already a flame of any kind in the house; that would have been rank extravagance.

Also during the afternoon, Mother would make a big batch of taffy and roast peanuts or parch a bowl full of corn. Father spent most of the day looking after the stock and firing up the stoves with plenty of comment on the weather. I remember Mother saying that she would like to see it snow once more like it used to in Indiana when it would come down gently in great, soft flakes. It would stay on most of the winter. This blizzard, however, distressed her.

By morning the wind had laid and the sun came out in all its brilliance. During the night, the snow had drifted even with the south end of the house being up to the gable, shutting out the light from the window! In many places between our house and the school, Father knew there would be high drifts as elsewhere in the district and that it would be useless to try to make it. So we had another day at home, which I thought was not going to be so much fun—until Father said, "All hands chip in, and we'll make a tunnel."

With shovels, big and little, we began on the drift next to the house, keeping close to it. By and by, we made it to the window (which was Father's goal in the first place, to clear it of snow). Then we went on through. Though the sun shone, it was very cold. It was so cold that the drift became crusted over. We dug back under a short distance and behold—we had a house like the Eskimos. Making a snowman and his wife took up the rest of the spare time for the day.

On the next day, the snow crust had frozen so hard that Father fixed the bobsled and away we went to school—right over those drifts with the horses not even breaking through. I bet you don't believe that!

In March, we had a round with another storm. Father had gone for a few days to help a neighbor with some carpentry, about five miles south of the schoolhouse. And for some reason, he had walked. The day when the work was finished was mild enough, and as he estimated that he would surprise us children by getting to the schoolhouse about four o'clock and walking home with us. He was not far on his way when he noticed that the wind had shifted to the north and was colder. By the time he had covered another mile, the snow had begun to fly with the sky looking heavier and darker all the time. He quickened his steps almost into a run; he knew he had little time to spare. Against the cold, piercing wind with the blinding snow, it was hard to make headway or estimate how far he had gone.

Eventually, he reached the schoolhouse. It was locked. The very thought of the children out in this storm made him sick at heart. The only comforting thought was that the teacher would be with them. Though he could see very few feet ahead of him, he knew that he had no time to lose. Every few steps, he would call out and listen. With no sound but the whistling wind in return, he would push on, not always sure that he was pushing on in the right direction. The snow had become deep, especially in drifts through which he would flounder, being very careful not to lose his sense of direction. And all this time, he was becoming more and more exhausted. Once a dim shadow of what seemed to be a soddy loomed before him, but it was obscured the next instant by the whirling snow. A few more dragging steps, and there it was. His first thought was whether the children were safe inside. Then he saw Mother run out to close the chicken house door and hurry back into the house. He called to her, but his voice was thrown back by the wind.

They're safe, or Mother wouldn't be thinking about chickens, he thought. Relieved of that great anxiety and in sight of the house, Father let himself sink into a great snow drift (to rest a moment). As he relaxed, he began to drift off into sleep. All at once, he thought, *I'm freezing to death!*

With one great effort, he took the few remaining steps and, with hand on the latch, he fell in the doorway. One can imagine what a commotion there was. We packed his hands and feet in snow to take out the frost and Elizabeth hurried to make him some potato soup.

"I could never understand until now why men have been frozen to death so near home," Father said. "I just gave up when I saw the house and felt that the children were safe."

The teacher thought that a storm was coming and had dismissed us at noon. No experience on the prairie is more vivid to me than this, and I suppose it's because it was so frightening. I was completely subdued, and I'm sure I didn't try to shirk my share of the dishwashing that night!

The storm raged on through the night and the next day, clearing by that following evening. And by the morning after the storm, the settlers were making their way from one place to another to see if all was well with their neighbors. Some had lost stock but, fortunately, all of the people in our neighborhood were safe.

So much late snow was a forerunner for a good wheat crop, providing there had been enough moisture in the fall to be able to sow it. And that year, there had been. So when the huge snow piles disappeared, the wheat was green and gave promise of a big crop, which we ended up having. The wheat matured before the hot winds really had a chance to ruin it.

Father had sown many acres of corn, and Mother had planted a lovely garden, which was flourishing. The wheat was cut, and threshers came (which was always a great day for us children). All was green and beautiful in the valley, except the yellow stubble of the wheat field where the cattle had been turned to graze.

STORMS AND FIRE

By July, the sun was hot; nary a cloud floated under the sun to give us a bit of shade, and the wind blew hotter than you can believe—if you have never been parched by one. The bare ground around the house would be too hot for our bare feet to endure by the afternoon. The green of the pastures turned to brown, and the ground cracked open, asking for a drink. The wind and heat continued day after day and week after week. Mother saw her garden wither and die.

One day, Father came in with a blade of corn from his field and rubbed it into powder between his palms and said, "Well, she's gone for this year, but we've got the wheat and the cattle and the chickens. And next year, we will have a big crop like we had the first year."

"Maybe, but not likely," said Mother. "It doesn't know how or when to rain in this country. It waits until everything is burned up. Or it comes as wind and hail and beats everything to pieces."

Mother was about right too. Many times when we so needed rain, we would watch the great, dark clouds gather on the southwest horizon, mounting higher and higher. And with the terrific lightning and thunder, it seemed that we could not possibly escape a good rain.

Before we children could recognize it, Father would say, "It's just wind," or "Well, she's going to pass us up this time." Sometimes it didn't pass us up. It would come with such a roar and a bang and so quickly that, even before we could get all of the little chickens in their coops, we would have to dash into the house in the midst of an apparent cloudburst.

His next outcry would be, "Here's a leak! Bring a pan!" Then "Here's another one!" and so on until there were no more pans. When the water went "ping-ping-ping" (drops instead of a steady stream), we knew the rain was about over.

We usually made for the little draw, which was a small stream that formed not far east of the house when it rained. We were not allowed to go to the big draw, still farther east, for the water was deeper there and ran swifter. Mother gathered an apron full of half-grown, drowned chickens after such storms to try to revive them. She saved a great many, but how I do not know.

At supper, two laws were laid down. Mother said that Father had to add more clay to the roof immediately to prevent more leaks. Father said that we children were to stay off the top of the house, since our being up there had more or less caused the leaks. The soddies had to have roof repairs every so often. Joe, Bill, and I felt the blow when Father gave us that stern, straight look with no smile in it. One of our favorite games had gone to pot!

By climbing on top of the cyclone cave adjoining the house at the back, we could by certain toeholds reach the eaves and then on over to the roof. And we were armed with what you would never believe: fishing tackle. Just the two of us would be on top at a time, hang our legs over the edge, and let down our lines. The third child would be down where we had assembled a pile of any old thing that would hang on a fish hook. Oh the talk and big fish tales that were wafted into that hot air! When we had "fished out" the imaginary pond, the "fish" would be thrown down. The one on the ground would come up, one of us on the roof would go down, and the game would go on.

For many weeks after the garden and the corn had been dried up, the hot winds continued to blow. Everything was so dry that there was a fear in every settler's heart of a prairie fire. At night when the wind had died down to a mere breeze, we could see here and there across the prairie thin lines of flame where people were burning their fireguards. Father had plowed his fireguards in the spring but had not yet burned the strip of grass left between the two rows of furrows. So one evening, we all set out to burn it. We took the wagon and a half-barrel of water, gunnysacks, and buckets to put out the fire should it leap across the plowed barrier. And with each one of us armed with a wet sack, watching our own particular section, Father watched all.

We were always sniffing the air, which so often was hazy and contained a faint odor of smoke.

"Just somebody burning fireguards," Father would say. "And probably sixty miles away—this wind would bring the smoke here in no time."

One morning soon after breakfast, Father said, "I don't like the looks of that sky in the south, and that smell of smoke in the south is pretty strong. And with this high wind ... well, I'm going to round up the cattle and get them into the corral. While I'm doing that, you folks draw plenty of water for the house, fill the horse tubs at the well, and get several buckets and sacks to have them ready. Unless I'm sadly mistaken, that's not fireguard smoke!"

By the time the cattle were safe in the corral, there was no question about the fact that the prairies were on fire.

"I'll go out and meet it; the neighbors will need my help."

Father and Mother lifted the tub half full of water into the wagon and loaded in the sacks and buckets. While he hitched up the horses, Mother had lunch and a jug of water ready for him. Father said he thought the guards would hold, but if the flames leaped them, we were to get into the house, stay, and not worry about him. We knew of a man who, just the year before, lost his life in a prairie fire not too distant from our home. We watched him go over the rise toward Duncan's and, in no time at all, watched him with many other fighters come over the rise, fighting that line of flame and smoke, which often hid the men from view. The flame would burn low as it devoured the powder-dry buffalo grass, and then leaped to a height of ten to fifteen feet when it came to a patch of blue stem or a drift of tumbleweed.

The men were working desperately, hauling water and taking turns flaying the flames. By the time the flames neared our place, the wind had shifted slightly to the southeast, which drove the fire almost parallel with the fireguard. So there was no trouble about the guard not holding. Our building and stocks were safe, but the fire swept on toward our neighbors. On its way, it burned over the west half of our claim not protected by guards. It was late evening when Father, worn out and black with grime, drove in to tell us that the fire was out, but it took the Pawnee to finally quench it.

He was too tired to talk, but when he had washed, changed his clothes, and eaten, we began to fire so many questions at him that he began with a stern, "What have I told you would happen if you ever played with fire!"

Looking through us, he drove the lesson home. Apparently, the Bates children had emptied some hot ashes and, finding a live coal, thought they would play at making a live campfire with straws for sticks. And no sooner was it ablaze then the wind landed the fire on their haystack. At that moment, the fight was on. There was no stopping it. They lost their hogs, hay, and chicken house—as well as the best part of their pasture.

When he felt we were sufficiently impressed, he went on with the happenings of the day. He told us what everyone had lost, whether in hay, stock, or buildings, and how hard all the men and women had worked. As he talked, we all felt so sorry for the Bates family, who had lost so much and had been the cause of all that trouble for the whole settlement.

The most distinct recollection of the part that I played in the fire story, aside from helping to hitch the horses to the wagon, was that when the flames were closest, I told Joe that we had better hide somewhere. He agreed and suggested we get under an old piece of carpet that we usually played on out in the yard. We ducked our heads and went under. But not for long because we just couldn't miss too much. And after a few peeps out, we saw that the danger had passed. We went sightseeing over to the edge of the burned area. In the years that we were there, that was our only experience with a prairie fire.

We never had a cyclone in Kansas, believe it or not! Several times, however, Mother hustled us down into the cave when those terrific blue-black clouds began to roll toward us, and the thunder seemed to split our ears. I always took my doll since I didn't mind the dark so much when I held her in my arms and felt my way to the molasses keg, which made an excellent seat for us while we waited out the storm. Mother would stand at the door and, after a time, she would open it a little to peer out to see if the house was still there. It always was. She would open the door wider, slip up into the kitchen to look out the window, and then tell us we could come on up. We would run and caper in the cool air—or perhaps cram our mouths full of hail and wiggle our toes in the mud. We accepted with glee whatever that old black, terrifying cloud had dealt us. Whatever it was, it was a change from the summer day-to-day monotony, and we welcomed it.

Speaking of change, our section of the West was beginning to experience a very definite change because of drought, almost total, for the third successive year. Added to that were the increasing hold of monopolies and big-moneyed interest upon the nation's economy. Money was tight. Farmers and townspeople in the new country had borrowed money on their property, expecting sufficient income to pay off the loans; when the drought-parched fields yielded no income to pay taxes and interest on the borrowed money, the banks refused to extend the loans. You can guess what happened next in the "short-grass country." Nearby and on distant horizons could be seen covered wagons—and this time they were headed east! Starved out!

Mother got five cents a dozen for eggs, and her delicious butter brought ten cents a pound! But calico was five cents a yard. Hard times was the topic of the day.

HARD TIMES CALL FOR HARDER WORK

It was being conceded by everyone that winter wheat or cattle, and on a large scale, were the only profitable enterprises for that section of the West. Therefore, the man who could operate only on a small scale had to get out or else.

Father decided he would not get out or starve either, for a while at least, even though he was a "small man." Then the cattle men began to take over the abandoned claims, usually by fair means, and their herds increased. They began to want better houses and room for their cowhands. Here was Father's chance. The new towns that had sprung up so quickly were dying just as suddenly. They were almost ghost towns. Empty dwellings and store buildings glared without shade in the burning hot winds that whirled dust through the unpaved streets. These buildings could be bought for an amazingly small sum; cattlemen were buying them, tearing them down, hauling the lumber to their ranches, and building themselves "frame" houses (which had been the dream of every soddy housewife). In turn, the soddy was fitted up for a bunkhouse.

When this process of dismantling the towns began, and before it had gone very far, Father approached the ranchers with the proposition of moving their houses intact on "skids" that he would make from the heaviest lumber. He showed them how it would save time, labor, and expense; the ranchers were so taken with the idea that he got several contracts within a few weeks. As nearly as I can remember, he made the skids out of 3x8s, laying them flat upon another and bolting them together until he had the required thickness and length. Only two skids were needed for small houses and three for the larger ones. It took two teams for each skid—one at each end of the skid after it had been pulled into position under the jacked-up house. When the skids were in position, the wagons with running gear only were wheeled into position. The end of the skid was fastened to the coupling pole with heavy log chains. Only the stoutest wagons could be used, and Father would carefully inspect every spoke, hub, and timber on them before they were put in place. It catastrophic to have a wagon break down. This would happen occasionally, causing much delay and extra expense. When all was ready, the horses would be hitched to their wagons and a rancher's house would be on the way, finally reaching its destination with no more harm done than the plaster cracked and fallen in several places, the windows having been removed and carefully stacked inside.

I wish I knew how many of those houses he moved. One he carted over the prairies for fifty miles. The work paid off; he came home after one such trip and announced that the next house-moving he did would be for us since he had just bought two houses in Kalvesta! We were ever so excited. One was a small store building but tall enough to be made into a two-story, which he expected to do, and the other was a two-room house that he planned to set back of the other to form a T-shape, with a porch on each side. He paid forty dollars for the store and twenty-five dollars for the dwelling, and he hauled them six miles. He was too busy to start remodeling, but we could see our own frame house in the offing. How we romped and played in those houses!

After so long a time, there came a lull in the house-moving business. Cattle were brought in from the south by the hundreds to be pastured on the rich buffalo grass. They required no other food. So for us, times became hard again. Though we had several acres in wheat, Father had to find carpenter work now and then in the community or by going to Jetmore.

When he would leave town for work, we were lonely without him; we missed his singing and his constant good humor and optimism. Mother was half-afraid and would bolt the doors at night as if to make amends. Seeing that she had made us a little frightened, she would do some extra thing, if no more than to sit with her sewing and tell us tales of her childhood. Her life had been so different than ours was. We thought of Indiana as a strange and beautiful land filled with great shady trees, wide rivers, and apple orchards everywhere with more fruit than could be eaten—where rain always came when needed, and there were no hot winds to dry up the garden—and there were uncles and aunts and cousins all over the place. To my mind, I thought it must be much lovelier than heaven. Sometime when we were all ears listening to her, a wild howl outside would freeze us with fear!

"Coyotes!" we would all whisper.

"They're after the chickens," Mother would say, "but they'll have no luck, for I shut them up tight."

Before the coyote could send out another hair-raising wail, old Tige would growl and send him flying off to join the howling pack that we could hear in the distance. Tige knew better than to chase him; the coyote would be a quarter of a mile away before he could get his legs untangled!

There was no reason for us to be afraid of coyotes; it was just that their high-pitched prolonged wail sounded so unearthly in the great silence around us. But one day we had a real experience with those prairie wolves. Father came home at noon, having finished a job for a neighbor, all excited, feeling sure that he had found a coyote's den about four miles away. He excited Joe and me by saying that we could go with him to dig into it. If there were young coyotes, there would be money. There was a bounty of two dollars for each scalp, and he might get a crack at the old one, but he doubted that. We piled into the wagon along with the pick, spade, shovel, a gunnysack, and the trusty old shotgun that was loaded and ready for action. Old Sam and Mart began trotting away, carrying us upon a new adventure.

The hole was in a small area where the ground was rough with gravelly banks. Father stopped the team in a level place a hundred yards perhaps from the hole. Helping with the tools, we hurried to the spot that Father pointed out. We saw chicken bones and a few feathers that were caught in weeds too tightly for the wind to blow them out. The mouth of the hole was worn slick—all signs that the coyotes were there.

We watched breathlessly as the dirt and gravel began to fly under Father's pick and spade. Digging back into the bank and a little downward, it was not long until he had dug quite a large hole. He listened and then told us to listen. We could hear them! As he continued to dig, he told us to be on the lookout for the old one, which we did, though not a trace of her could we see. When he lifted out a shovel of dirt, there was a mass of furry, wiggling little coyote puppies—And of all sights for our eyes, so many we couldn't count them. They were crawling and tumbling all over each other! Joe and I were down into that hole in a minute, each grabbing a puppy, and all three of us were talking at once. Father said we'd put them in the gunnysack and count them as we put them in, but we had left the sack in the wagon. He said he would go get it while we had a bit more play with them.

It seemed that he had just left us when we heard him yell at the top of his voice; a minute later, there was the roar of the shotgun. We popped up and out and wanted to know what had happened. He pointed and, a few feet away, the old coyote was dead. He had just reached into the wagon for the sack and turned to come back and saw her coming like a streak from the opposite direction—headed straight for the den. With the gun, he ran and shouted, but on she came. He had a fleeting vision of her throwing herself upon us, and when he knew he was near enough to shoot, he prayed the shot would strike the target—and it did!

"She would have torn you to pieces," he said, shaking his head. It made us pretty sober, too, and took much of the fun out of the adventure for the moment. Our spirits rose when we held the sack open and Father dropped them in one by one and counted up to ten!

As I think of it now, it seems that we should have been at least a little sorry for the poor little animals, with their Mother dead and left behind scalped, and knowing that they would soon be killed. But we were wild with glee when we rushed in to tell Mother that we had a sack full of coyotes, twenty dollars-worth besides the scalp of the old one.

Father dumped them all out on the kitchen floor for Mother, Elizabeth, and little Bill to see. They began to crawl in every direction, whimpering as they went. Mother had seen all of them that she wanted to and was not so fond of them being in her kitchen. She promptly ordered us all out with them. Joe thought he would like to keep one for a pet, but Father talked him out of the idea. I don't recall the argument used. That's the very last thing I remember about those coyotes. I know I didn't see them killed, but I don't know how he did it.

I've heard Father tell that story many times—and how much that money meant to him just then. Somehow I felt myself very much of a heroine, having escaped being pounced upon by a coyote in her den.

HOME REMEDIES

We children of the prairies were not afraid of anything, during the day at least, and ran around like wild things, venturesome as could be. It's a wonder that I ever lived to tell this tale. We, like the others out there, must have had a strong sense of self-preservation and knew how to apply it or else our guardian angel never took her eyes off us.

To illustrate, the roof of John Dickerson's stone house had fallen in, leaving the walls with the gable ends pointing upward. Playing about it one day, Joe began to climb the rough wall like a lizard and was soon on top. And not to be outdone, I was in a jiffy up there with him. But he, not content with just sitting there, jumped up and began to run around the wall, not stopping at the gables. He was scrambling up from one stone to another until he sat upon the top, bantering with me to follow. I took up the chase and away we went, up and down and around the top of that wall, gables and all! The angel surely had hold of our hair that time. And that was the only time Mother had seen us and laid down the law when we got home, and there was no more gable chasing!

Aside from fearing that in our escapades we would fall in the well or that while loping over the prairies we would be bitten by a rattlesnake, Mother didn't worry much about us. We were pretty leery about the well ourselves, but the rattlers didn't tell us anything; we were on to their technique, knowing that they would not strike unless they were coiled—and we could pretty much depend upon their rattle as a warning that they were near. If coiled, and ready to strike, we would throw a stick, stone, or even some twisted weeds at him at a safe distance, of course, to get him to strike and thus straighten out. Then old Tige would dash at him before he could coil again, grabbing him in the middle, Tige would shake and crush it until the dead snake was ready for us to take by the tail and drag home. Once or twice, Joe and I killed one while playing down by the stone quarry with broken stone. We always took them to the house so Father could cut off the rattles; we kept them as souvenirs. By the time that we left the claim, we had nearly a matchbox full.

Once, when we were not so far from the house, Mother heard Joe yelling at the top of his voice and saw me bending over him. A snake was the first thing that came to her mind, and she was sure he had been bitten by one. So grabbing her little bottle of whiskey from her medicine box, she ran as fast as she could make it to where we were, only to find that he had stepped into the middle of a ball-cactus bed. Several of the marble-sized spiny balls had broken loose and were still sticking in his foot.

White with fear and panting for breath, she said, "Joe, I've got a notion to spank you good, for you nearly scared me to death!"

And with that, he howled all the louder and said, "I wasn't callin' you; I was callin' Tige."

Tige would pull the cactus balls from our feet as he did from his own. He would curl up his lip so as not to get pricked, then very carefully partially close his mouth over the ball and gently pull it out, then lick our feet as he did his! No wonder that we loved that dear old dog Tige! Mother soon had them out to the tune of screeches and sobs from poor little Joe; those barbs were as painful coming out as they were going in.

The whiskey was set back in the medicine box and ready for duty should there be another snake scare. Mother's medicine box was not to be touched for in it she had remedies for all our ills—from stomachache to fever. Many of the prescriptions she had brought from Indiana from her doctor, besides herbs from the big woods and her mother's garden. Teas and salves, mustard plasters, sulfur, sugar (not the usual molasses), and asafetida were tied in little bags to be hung around our necks in winter to ward off colds. I could stand most of it except that terribly bitter tansy tea! Whatever was the matter with me that I had to take it, I don't know. But I'll never forget the taste.

She had a concoction that we called the "hot medicine," and was it hot! And did it ever cure our stomachaches. It was equal parts of camphor, rhubarb, capsicum, and laudanum. A teaspoon in sweetened water was the dose; in five minutes, we were good as new and "rarin' to go!" I doubt whether a druggist would fill that today; capsicum is red pepper—and laudanum is opium! For fear you might want to try it sometime, don't take my word that the dose was a teaspoonful. It may have been a certain number of drops. I am positive as to the ingredients; however, I used to sing them off while Mother fixed the dose.

Her remedies were potent or else the climate was all that could be desired for good health; in the seven years that we lived out there, we had a doctor only once and that was when Father had the grippe (same as influenza now). He had a bad cold and became delirious one night.

He said, "Get the stove poker and kill the teakettle."

Mother began to work on him in real earnest; by the time it was light, she sent Elizabeth on Sam to a neighbor to go for a doctor. By the time the doctor arrived, Mother had the fever down, but he was very weak and sick for several days. Being a member of the Odd Fellows Lodge, two of the brothers came to see him; when they were leaving, they asked him if there was something that he would like, especially to eat. Of all things, he said gooseberry pie! The next day they brought in the gooseberries—the first that we had ever seen.

Fruit of any kind was scarcer than rain out there. It was store-dried apples or dried peaches or sorghum for sweets. I preferred the sorghum to the fuzzy peaches or the apples with a part of the cores left in. Mother looked at them pretty carefully though, and her dried apple pies never went begging. They were good.

Some seasons we went to the Pawnee for wild grapes and chokecherries, which were transformed into grape butter and cherry preserves to be kept for company. When we were hard up for sweets, Mother would make egg butter by beating an egg or so. She would add boiling syrup and continue beating until it was light and thick, and then flavor it strongly with lemon. She would always pour it into the large stemmed preserve dish that Joe has. Most of the grownups were fond of it, but I was not.

As I've gone along, I haven't said much about the teachers who, for four to six months out of the year, were members of our family. They were all good sports and took everything in their stride, helping with the work occasionally. They were much company for us when Father was away for any length of time. Many years after, when I was living in Larned, I met with Mr. Ruff. I asked him what he remembered most about his stay.

He said, "It was your mother's ability to set good meals with so little to do with. I especially remember that egg butter. It was good!"

Then he told about her parching wheat and grinding it as a substitute for coffee. When we ran out of coal oil, she would twist a small piece of cloth and place it in a saucer of melted lard; after lighting the end on the rim, we would have a light (a Betty lamp, in the antique language). I remembered those things when he spoke of them.

BEAUTY FROM THE DIRT

Most of the charm of pioneering is in the tales written about it for those in comfortable circumstances to read. There are two things that make it bearable: dreams and the heart-touch of those passing through the same experience. We had such good friends out there; every time a family gave up and went back East, we felt a bit lonelier. Day by day, the dreams that my parents had were growing dimmer.

"It was not a farming country," they conceded. It was for cattle only—and cattle in a big way. The apple orchard Father had so carefully planted and tended refused to grow beyond small shrub size. When its one little apple withered and dropped, his hopes for a fine farm home dwindled to nothing. He brought in cattle to graze on the homestead quarter and the "preemption" quarter adjoining. That provided a small income.

I recall one quite large herd from Texas or Oklahoma—steers with horns. The owner wanted them dehorned and was trying to find someone to do the job. Father volunteered at eight and a third cents per head. Getting the contract immediately, he set to work building the dehorning chute, which was merely a narrow sled with heavy runners, high sides, and slide fasteners at the back and one in front to prevent the animal from moving on through, then one to slide across above the neck to hold the head secure while the horns were sawed off. There was a man or so to help, and it was not many days until the herd was hornless.

Other ranchers, hearing that he had the equipment, asked him to come dehorn their cattle. And thus he entered a new business—one that he didn't like. It was cruel and very hard, exhausting work. I've heard

THE CRAZY QUILT OF LIFE

him say that, after a day of it, he was in a state of weak trembles. Strong man that he was, but from ranch to ranch, old Sam and Mart pulled the chute until the last herd was dehorned. The last herd was a large one, and the owner refused to pay him but five cents a head when the job was completed, saying he had heard of a man who was charging only that! In those days, Father on occasion could use pretty strong language, and that was an occasion! Father just "laid him out."

Running cattle on the place called for a little herding, though not much more than heading them off when they strayed too far away. That was an easy task when Sam was at home to ride. Otherwise, we were out for a long run every once in a while. Straight running always gave me a pain in my side, so I developed sort of a crazy springing lope, which was fun and carried me over the ground much faster.

One day, a man in a "surrey with the fringe on top," came driving up to see his cattle. With him was his little girl about my age. She was all dressed up, as was her father. "Lawyer Fuller" lived about halfway toward Jetmore. Since Father was not at home, I volunteered to direct him to where the cattle were. I started off on a lope, telling him to follow. By the time he had turned around, I was well ahead of them. And knowing that I would have to sprint some to keep ahead of the horses, I fairly flew.

The horses came faster and Mr. Fuller called, "Hold on. Come and ride!"

I was dumfounded. Into a surrey I climbed, barefooted, suntanned, and my hair wind-blown and blousy, a study in contrast with dainty Ellen. What a ride that was! I doubt that any since has ever so thrilled me. We thought that our spring-wagon was pretty fancy, but a surrey was "just out of this world." The one point that saved my pride, if I had any, was that I had on my favorite flowered dress, pale blue, with yellow daisies and pink primroses scattered over it. When it was my turn to have a new dress, I always said, "Bring me a new dress with flowers on it." Father always tried to fill the order.

From spring through summer, the prairies were highlighted with many lovely flowers, which were a joy to my heart. The one I loved was what we called wild moss, a low-growing perennial with magenta blossoms on six-inch stems. The flower resembled rose moss, but it was somewhat larger.

LIDA BEATY-JACKSON

It grew in patches often ten feet across—and how they did brighten up the landscape!

I had not seen any since leaving the West. However, in 1926, we went to the Limberlost Cabin of Gene Stratton Porter, where the governor accepted the estate for the State of Indiana. In wandering around the grounds, I came upon a patch of it! It was like meeting an old friend, and I immediately located Mr. Porter to ask about it. He told me it was low poppy mallow; he later sent me some seed. As I write, there are some of those magenta stars in the garden.

There was another wild mallow that was very sweet. It was like a tiny hollyhock, perhaps eight to ten inches high, with brick-red flowers growing around the stem exactly. There were patches of what must have been wild larkspur, though I have never been able to find a description in any wildflower book. It was white and rather fuzzy with a touch of black on the "spur." To us they were elephant trunks!

Down by the stone quarry, there were Johnny-jump-ups (violets), and on the rougher ground were the stately yucca, commonly called soap-weed and bear grass. The sunflowers were ever-present, though I never heard them referred to as a nuisance, and it was fun to watch them turn to face the sun. Most of them were well-branched and really pretty. There were great beds of prickly pear, covered with golden blossoms, and the smaller varieties of cacti with their starry red blooms were to be admired, hands off. They were always ready to defend themselves with a thousand spears. There was a dainty orange wild dahlia as well. The blue vervain and the purple gay-feather we classed as weeds and didn't gather, but we would have the butterfly-weed with its orange panicles. Mother said they were full of chiggers, so the "chigger-weed" was taboo.

We were ordered not to touch the beautiful lavender loco with its silvery leaves. It was very poisonous to cattle, and it went without saying that it might not be too healthy for us. There was one pretty trumpet-shaped yellow and brown flower that we had little to do with because of its bad odor; the plant had a clammy, sticky feeling when touched. I've never learned the name, but we called it "devil's claw" because of the hard seed pod with two very sharp claws on one end.

As I've written, many of these flowers have come to mind that I have not thought of since leaving there. It's almost as if they popped up and said, "Don't forget me!" I was just about to forget perhaps the dearest flower of the prairies: the "sensitive rose." It grew on a prickly vine. The leaves were compound and very fragile. They were so sensitive that, when we touched them, the leaflets would close together! Of course we touched them to see the fun, knowing that they would open again later. The "roses" were little balls of pink, about the size of a marble and resembled a ball tassel on a baby shoe, yet each tiny erect antler was tipped with a ball of yellow pollen. How dainty and how fragrant! The stems were rarely longer than three inches; most were too short to be gathered except in small bouquets of three or four. Many years later, I learned that they were mimosas. They were also called "Snow in the Mountain" because each green leaf, edged with white, could grow two feet in the rough places. It was quite pretty in a bouquet of color, though the milky juice that ran from the stems when picked was not so pleasant. In this case of naming the flowers, the "first shall be last," for with the first breath of spring came the tiny salt and pepper, nestled down in the curls of the buffalo grass as if afraid there might be another blizzard. It was well named; the composite blossom looked very much like a mixture of salt and pepper. It was a sure sign that prettier posies were on the way.

Yes, the prairies offered many things of interest to a child—and one to be remembered was the miracle of the mirage. To the west and south, the heat shimmered in waves on the distant horizon. Built in their reflections were a water tower, a fencepost, and tall forests of weeds. Quite often, we could see Kalvesta reflected in the air and the usual lakes of blue water. The mirages were a phantom end toward which the tired and thirsty pioneers pushed on and on to end in great disappointment.

OLD CLEOPATRA AND CHEAP JIM

A great day it was when "Cheap Jim" came in sight over the ridge. He had a regular route that he covered once a year, and it was always when summer was its hottest that he appeared at our house in his funny little covered wagon drawn by a white mule. He was a peddler, and a colorful one at that, which undoubtedly made up a good part of his stock and trade. He had decorated Old Cleopatra's harness with pompoms of red and yellow tissue paper with smaller ones on the tips of her huge, floppy ears. And not only was the mule decorated, but buttons, badges, pins, ribbons, and even beads adorned the front of Cheap Jim's shirt in great variety and profusion.

Father would tease him and ask him if he had been fighting more battles since he had more or different buttons. The little old man would say, "Yis, yis! Got buttons all over me, but I never fighta."

Nobody but himself knew the why of all this decoration. I think he must have been Italian and just loved color. A bright yellow silk kerchief was knotted about his neck and, above that, a round, ruddy face, pierced with sparkling black eyes, then a fringe of hair, and last, a bald crown to cap the strange little figure. He would hop out of his wagon with a loud "Helloa," and then "Wanna by any-ting today?" Then he would start to advertise. "Got justa whatcha need. Needles, pins, washboards, monkey wrenches, thread, nails, calico, matches, buttons, wash pans, beads, combs," and on until he had mentioned every item in the entire wagon—even though the folks would from the beginning shake their heads. And when he was through naming his inventory, folks would say, "Nothing today, Jim," as if to make it final. But Jim was not near through.

"Cheap, cheap," he would cry. Taking one article after another, he would comment upon its worth—and how much cheaper it was than any stores would sell it. When still there was no sale, he would begin cutting his price and continue until he had it down to about what we could buy it for in the stores. All of which we knew he would do, and he knew it better than we did. It was only for bare necessities that we would part with the scarce dimes at our house. Once when he seemed so disappointed that the folks didn't buy more, they asked him to rest and stay for dinner since it was nearly noon. And with a grin, he started to unhitch Old Cleopatra almost before Father had the words out of his mouth.

"We won't have so much," he said, "but Elizabeth will make a big pan of her good biscuits, and that will set you off feeling a lot better." Elizabeth made great biscuits. In fact, she was a splendid cook. She and Mother soon had a nice meal on the table, topped off with wild grape butter and watermelon preserves. These last two items I know she had for she never failed to have a supply put back for company and dished them out no matter who the company was.

It was my turn to keep the flies off the table, so I armed myself with the "fly brush" (fringed paper on a long stick) and took up my position opposite the guest so I wouldn't miss a word he said. I remember not a word, but I do remember how he fell upon those biscuits, taking one every time that Father did. And that was often, let me tell you. I was glad when they were through because I was relieved of my job minding the flies. Nobody had screens, and when the cooking began, the flies came rolling in from the barn lot. They were shooed from the food while it was being prepared and eaten. Then after the dishes were done, each would get a paper or towel and round them up and out of the open door in swarms and the hot winds would sail them away. Oh how we ran for the swatter when one stray fly wandered in. I doubt there was a single case of illness out there due to flies. We were all a healthy lot. Of course, everyone had a mosquito net, which was to keep the flies, not mosquitoes, from the babies as they slept. We had no mosquitoes there.

Cheap Jim soon made ready to move on after thanking the folks again and again for his dinner. When the old mule was treated to another good drink and hitched up, the little old peddler called Elizabeth and me to the wagon. And handing her a pretty string of beads, he said, "These for the good beeskits." To me, he gave a pair of black lace mitts and then said, "And these for shooing the flies from me bald head so I could eat the beeskits!" Then he laughed and, with many motions, tried to express his gratitude as he drove away.

We were overwhelmed that he would give us such lovely gifts for so small a favor. The mitts were also called half-hands, there being no fingers in them. Mine fit well, so I put them on and paraded around with them, carrying my little beaded bag, thinking I had all I needed for a finished costume. But I, so browned by the hot winds, must have surely appeared ludicrous flaunting all that finery!

TIME FOR A CHANGE

Another winter at the end of a season of drought, with no work in sight locally, the folks decided to give it up. I remember so well hearing Father say, "I'm tired of living in a country where my children can never see an apple growing on a tree." He decided to move to Jetmore for the time being and then he would "look around" for a permanent location. In Jetmore, he would find a little carpentry work and some odd jobs with the team.

There was much advertising being scattered abroad of southwest Missouri as "The Land of the Big Red Apples." Father had been looking over circulars that he had picked up in Jetmore until he had almost enough fever to make the flight, but he decided to consider it a little longer while we tarried in Jetmore.

We had twenty-four head of cattle—all of them were sold, except Old White Face—for $7.50 a head! We would take along White Face and our chickens. A pair of iron gray fillies was a perfect match, and he sold the spring wagon. And then we were ready to load up and leave the soddy as scores had done before us. The vision of fine farms had vanished into high, hot winds, carrying with it seven years of my parents' wasted energy. But I am left with many years of rich experience that I count as great treasure in my storehouse of memories.

There was one more thing—we must have a farewell party. It took the form of a supper to which all of the neighbors who were left were invited. It was not a real meal, being more of what was called a pie supper. Mother and Elizabeth were busy all day with pies and cakes. I remember little about it except that Father, having been to town, brought some red grapes. They were the first we had ever seen, and I saved some of mine for Jesse Mould, my boyfriend. We went outside to eat them in the dark where we would not be seen! Jesse was soon to leave for New York to live with an uncle who offered him an education.

Looking back across the stretch of fifty-two years to the leave-taking of the soddy for the much talked-of frame house in town, the thing that I remember most vividly, after the night of our party, was my farewell visit to the neighbors. As the good-byes were said to everyone, young or old, married or single, I gave a most pressing invitation to "stop at the little brown house just as you go in" when they made the next trip to Jetmore.

Alas for the folks, my invitations were certainly taken literally (though they would have come anyway) for we were scarcely settled until they began to come, singly and by whole families. We were glad to have them, of course, but I can see yet the worried look on Mother's face as she would call me and tell me to "go find Pa and tell him to bring some meat, for we had company for dinner." I can hear Father's exasperated remarks when he heard the news. We were in the midst of the panic of the early 1890s, and money for extra meals was scarce. Mother had a way of making a good meal out of so little, and we had our own milk and butter. By the time the meal was over, everybody (including Father) was in a grand mood, and all laughed at "the hard times."

Uncle Logue (Mother's brother), Aunt Lizzie, and their children, Pearl and Vernan, who had taken a claim near us just a year or two before, gave it up and moved to Jetmore at the same time that we did. There was little work to be had, but there was news that another Oklahoma Run would soon be staged by the government. Father and Uncle Logue decided it might be a good thing to get down there, stake a claim or town lot, and then sell it and make some money. That and the adventure was Father's idea as they set to work mantling once more the old wagon with its bows and cover, storing their camping equipment.

They made the run, and Father made enough to pay his expenses and was back in a few weeks. Uncle Logue stayed, having staked a claim on some lots near what is now Blackwell. He sent for his family, and I did not see Cousin Pearl again until last year (1939). She and her husband stopped to see us at Fairhill, en route home to Seattle from the World's Fair at New York! How we talked and talked, sometimes with misty eyes, as we traveled back and forth over those long years.

She had done well, married an insurance man, Herbert Ladley, in Oklahoma, and later went to the State of Washington. Her four lovely children have college educations and are doing well.

One of the first things that happened to me at Jetmore was to change my name from Eliza to Lida. On the first day I went to school, who should I see in my class but a Negro girl named Liza! Never having seen any Negroes, I was embarrassed beyond words that our names were so similar and hastily asked my teacher to call me something else at school. She readily agreed and idly jotted down a few names. For some reason or none, they all began with the letter L. Lida was the first, and I said that the first one would do since it would be used only in school hours. Lida it was and has been to this day; soon the home folks took it up, and I was Grandmother's namesake no longer (though I kept the middle name Ann). I have always so much regretted that I didn't just use the name Ann from the moment I thought it should be changed.

We soon felt at home in the county seat. Father was doing carpentry work, all of us children were in school, and Mother, Elizabeth, and I joined the Congregational church. We liked it very much. Elizabeth sang in the choir, and it wasn't long before I was chosen as the Sunday school librarian. When I was handed the key to that bookcase containing two or three hundred books, it was one of the proudest moments of my life. I could not understand then or since why I, such a newcomer, was chosen for what I considered a very important work. With the exception of my one little storybook, *Fine Feathers Don't Make Fine Birds*, that I had read perhaps a dozen times, I had not even seen any other story books—and now a world of delight had opened up before me. I made up my mind to read every book in that library, and I almost did!

I loved my church and our young minister, Mr. Hull, but I was not at all sectarian. On the Sundays that he preached elsewhere, after Sunday school, I would go over to the Methodists or Presbyterians in company of my dearest friend, Myrta Baugher, after which she usually would come home with me or I would walk the two miles home in the country with her. We were fast friends always, and our paths crossed at important times in later years. Now, at seventy-two, she sends me lovely messages. She lives in Lamar, Colorado, and is now Mrs. Albin.

But while I was "taking" to town civilization, I was pretty much a child of the open spaces, with country chores to do, often feeding the chickens, gathering the eggs, and always feeding and milking Old White Face. It was also my job to go with Joe to take her to the pasture that Father had rented west of town. On these excursions, to and from the pasture, we had various experiences, one of which I am ashamed to tell, but here it goes.

Within the pasture was a deserted old stone house with the windows out and the roof partly fallen in; it had been taken over by barn swallows. There were dozens of nests plastered along one side near the top—and what did we do but climb the rough wall and rob those nests! With hands full of eggs, we selected a target and blazed away. How many more swallows there would be today to devour harmful insects if we hadn't destroyed all those potential ancestors. That was a shameful deed! I am reminded of it every summer when the swallows come back to build in our old barn. We killed some snakes too and stretched them along the barbed wire fence, tying them fast with our shoestrings.

JETMORE

We lived in Jetmore for five years. It was a happy time for me. I made average grades in school, nearly flunking however, my arithmetic. But I was proud of my A's in geography. I read Scott and Dickens and other good works from our Sunday school library and was forever memorizing a "recitation" to be given on some program in one of the churches or in the courthouse. The only time that I ever claimed the distinction of being in a declamatory contest was while there.

The Women's Christian Temperance Union (W.C.T.U.) was having contests everywhere. Boys and girls were allowed to choose a selection from a booklet published by that organization, memorize it, and on a given night, judges would be appointed. And, to a full house, the speakers would contest for the silver medal. There were perhaps half a dozen of us; one in the group had tried twice before, and this would be her last chance. We all feared Carrie Sylvus, and our fears were well grounded; she won the medal! Her mother was a tireless worker in the organization, and it was nice that Carrie had the honor. I thought Myrta's boyfriend, Fred Sweet, should have had it. The name of my speech was "Two Fires."

> It was dark midnight in that city,
> And Sleep, that sweet goddess of Rest
> Kept guard in the hut and the mansion
> With its presence so restful and blest.
> When hark!

Well, the fire bells rang, and the city burned to ashes, as I remember. But that was nothing to the other raging fire that consumed the drunkard!

That night, there were gestures high and wide as we dealt a sledgehammer to the demon intemperance. I was in touch with that group for many years, and they grew into fine Christian men and women. Fred married Myrta and won a real prize.

Mr. Hull, our wide-awake minister, organized the young people of the town into a Bible study class, meeting one night a week in the schoolhouse with some of the young teachers enrolling. The course was on the life of the Apostle Paul.

Some time when you grandchildren read about that wonderful man and his great missionary journeys, you can say that your grandmother once won a prize on the story of Paul. The prize for the highest grade was a lovely story called "Titus." I had a hard time for a few days keeping in the proper spirit of humility, especially since my school teacher had been a competitor in the class! It was largely memory work, and the poor teacher had much more to do than I did. I have no doubt that all of my lessons suffered during that period. In retaliation, it is a wonder that he didn't flunk me!

In an all-school geography test, I also won a prize: Scott's *Ivanhoe*. I was so disappointed that I had already read the book!

You may be wondering what we did for amusement—with no radio, movie, or cars to chase around in. Was there no excitement out in that wind-blown town of the monotonous prairies? Compared to what I had previously experienced, there was. On moonlit nights, a group of us would go "tick-tacking." We would go quietly up to someone's house and then, at a signal from the leader, let out a terrible war whoop, or drag a stick down the weatherboarding, scaring the old people out of their rocking chairs—as well as out of their wits. Mother didn't approve of that game—and no wonder. I didn't get to go out often, even though it seemed to be an accepted game of the youngsters.

At the noon hours, we girls would hurry back from our lunch to gather around the school organ and sing old ballads as well as the popular songs. From the one piece of sheet music someone would have, we would copy the words in our notebooks that were kept for that purpose. I still have mine. Many of the popular songs of the day were handed down, such as "The Orphan Girl," "Barbara Allen," "Just Tell Them That You Saw Me," "Only a Bird in a Gilded Cage," "After the Ball," and "Take Back Your Gold for Gold Can Never Buy Me."

After more than sixty years, we are hearing again, over the radio, the songs we loved best because they were of our time and place. "Red River Valley," "The Dying Ranger," and for us there was real pathos in those words:

> O bury me not on the lone prairie
> Where the wild coyotes will howl o'er me,
> Where the rattle-snakes hiss and the wind blows free
> O bury me not on the lone prairie.

Then there were the birthday parties! I laugh to myself now when I remember how formal we tried to be with those invitations. On ruled tablet paper, we would write: "You are cordially invited to attend the birthday party of Lida Beaty on November the 19." Thus I wrote when I was fourteen. The paper was then folded over and over until an inch wide. Then, one end was folded cornerwise until it would lock and not come unfolded. Across the free section would be written the name of the guest and, at school, we would slip in at recess and lay them on each desk for the surprise element! What a gay time we had at that party. We started in with a quiet game of charades and then played musical chairs. We played "Miller Boy," "Skip to my Lou," and other dust-raising games until we were choked to the point of rushing outside for fresh air.

I recall that we had canned peaches and cake for refreshments and finished off with popcorn. After all had gone, I gloated over my pretty gifts: handkerchiefs, celluloid picture frames, a handkerchief box, and spiral white celluloid hair ornament, which topped the psyche knot into which I was trying to coax my skimpy yellow hair. I was particularly happy over two China silk handkerchiefs with scalloped edges in each corner and lightly colored embroidered flowers. These we knotted in the center and pinned them as a tie on our best dresses (I have two lovely ones purchased not long ago with some old materials which I will give to Caroline and Ann).

Elizabeth was such a fine sister. Mother was sick a great deal; so many of the home responsibilities fell upon her. At the time of my party, she worked so hard to have everything nice for me. The next winter, she was through school and was teaching in the country south of Jetmore; the following year, she taught at Hanston, a village you can find on the map.

Times were hard for us, and Father decided to run for probate judge, thinking that the salary would help to keep the wolf (coyote) from the door. He was pretty sure he would be elected, but he lost by two votes! How disappointed we all were, but I have heard him say many times afterward that it was the finest thing that could have happened to him. This caused him to decide to make a definite change. He asked Congressman Jerry Simpson for a job and came home with the news that he had been offered work at Osawatomie Mental Hospital as an attendant at twenty-five dollars a month with board, room, and laundry included. He was to report at once, which meant he was to take the train. The rest of us would follow in the covered wagon as soon as school was out, which, as I remember, was about a month or six weeks. The horses and wagon he had kept, so after making all the arrangements necessary, including the hiring of a Mr. Right to drive us through. His adventure in the West was over, and a new era in his life had begun.

The weeks ahead were busy ones for Mother. Elizabeth was away at teaching. With her gone, all the responsibility fell upon Mother to have things ready to move in a given time. Father had written, charting our course. If we departed on May 4, we should reach Osawatomie on the fourteenth. The night before our departure, the neighbors met us and gave us a farewell dinner. I remember the great quantities of chicken and cake that were brought and the good time we all had.

By ten o'clock the next morning, we were all loaded and ready to start. We traveled light; most of the goods had been sent on ahead. Mother thought it not quite proper that she should sit up on the spring seat with the driver, so she took her place back on the beds with pillows to support her as she leaned back against the wagon cover. We children took our turns in the seat. Joe, the twelve-year-old, thought he should be the most privileged to sit there since he helped take care of the horses and did considerable amounts of driving. We camped overnight in the outskirts of Larned, and I saw my first iris-flags, as Mother called them. I thought they were quite pretty, but they didn't appeal

THE CRAZY QUILT OF LIFE

to Mother at all. I was sure there must be something wrong with them; I had never seen a flower that she didn't like. Now I don't wonder; they were one of those old muddy yellows. I wish she were here to see my prizewinners in the garden now; she would love them. As we pulled out early the next morning, little did I think that in ten years I would return there to spend so many happy years—and because of circumstances in no way relating to our having been in western Kansas! And Margaret was born there.

For us children, the trip was a great adventure. Elizabeth and I would start a little ahead of the team so that we might explore the woods or fields for new flowers. She suggested that we get on from each county through which we passed and press them in a book for a souvenir of our trip. I still have the book.

One afternoon, we saw a heavy storm cloud in the west and watched it anxiously. The horses were urged on so that we might reach Salina and shelter for the night. But all too soon, the wind, lightning, and thunder were upon us and with such fury as only those Kansas plains can know. We were only a few hundred yards from an open barnyard gate, and the driver turned the horses to seek shelter by one of the farmer's large barns. No sooner had we entered than we were met by the irate farmer, waving us back most violently and shouting in broken English. He was a German settler and was communicating that we must drive on. Luckily we were already in, and our driver stood his ground. He said he would not take the family out against the storm—except at the point of a gun!

The pelting rain and the farmer's abusive words came down upon us with the roaring wind. Finally, and I suppose to get out of the storm himself, the old man said we could stay all night if we lit no fires and pulled out of there by daylight. As he ran to the house, we rushed into the barn. We were thankful to escape the fury of the storm.

For more than an hour, it seemed the roof would be lifted from over our heads as the thunder rolled and crashed. I went off alone in a hay-filled corner and prayed that we all might be spared. When the rain and wind slackened, Mother set out some cold food. After a snack, everyone except Mother brought our blankets in and slept on the hay. She climbed back into the wagon to rest on her featherbed, but "not to sleep," she said.

OSAWATOMIE

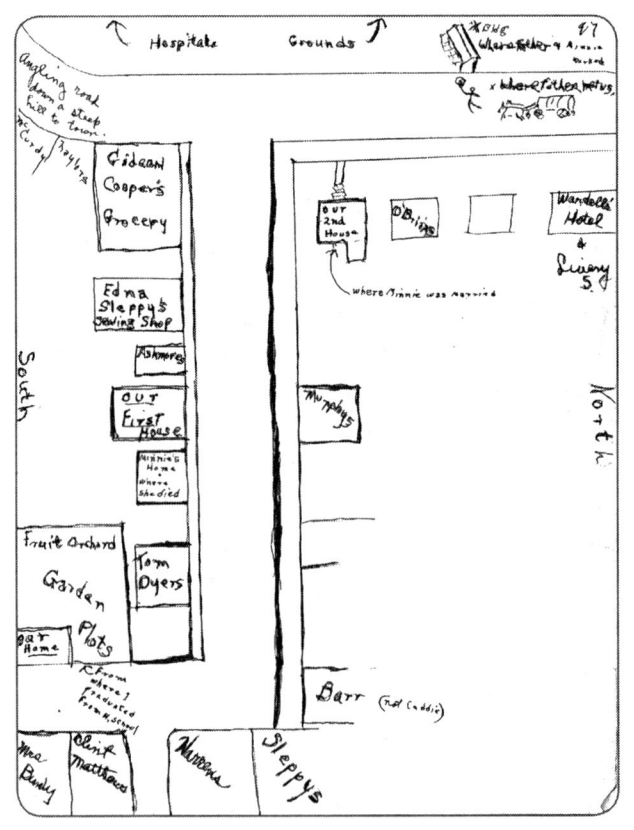

A hand-drawn map of Osawatomie

We were out and away at daybreak, not staying even long enough to thank our host for his hospitality! Father always wanted to go back there and give that man a trouncing. He had timed it right; we arrived at

Osawatomie on May 14, 1897. We came in from the north along the road that passed the hospital grounds.

Good fortune was with us in that Father was out on the grounds, giving his men an airing and watching for us. How happy he was as he hurried out to the road to meet us. Leaving his men to the care of an assistant, he went with us to the little house he had rented. Just down the street and around the corner, it was among a small group of houses east of the grounds rented almost exclusively to employees of the hospital. The town proper lay in the lowland a mile to the south across the Marais des Cygnes River, on a point of land between it and the Pottawatomie River where the two met to form the Osage River.

It is interesting to know that when the Miami and Pottawatomie Indians were herded out of Indiana, they were settled along these streams, thereby naming the county Miami and the river Pottawatomie, and the town a combination of the names of the tribes of the Osage and the Pottawatomie.

Osawatomie is of some historical interest from another angle. At the time we moved there, a log cabin stood a mile and a half west of town. John Brown helped to build it, and he used it as an underground station before the Civil War, helping the slaves to escape. Following is a copy of a statement concerning the building, written by C. S. Adair and signed by him:

> This is a history of the so-called John Brown's Cabin, or Kansas Home. The cabin was owned by Rev. S. L. Adair, a brother-in-law of John Brown. The logs of the back part were drawn together by John Brown with two yokes of oxen, were scored by Fredric Brown, son of John Brown, and were hewn by Henry Thompson, son-in-law of John Brown. In the back room, on Christmas day 1858, the largest part of the slaves taken out of Missouri, were concealed.

I knew the Adairs; one of the young lads was a pupil of mine later, and I was invited out to supper one evening. Walter's mother set the table in the cabin, a few steps from their home, thinking that I would appreciate the novelty of it, which I did very much from the historical standpoint.

Many years after, when I had moved away, the town set aside a section for a park, erected a statue of John Brown, and engaged Father to superintend the removal of the cabin from the country into the park where it now stands. In the reconstruction, there seemed to be an extra clapboard from the roof, and Father gave it to me. I still have it and will pass on to Jo since Osawatomie is her birthplace!

Theodore Roosevelt dedicated the park, making his initial speech to form the Progressive Party of which he was the titular head and upon which he ran for the presidency, being defeated by Woodrow Wilson, though he ran far ahead of Taft, the Republican nominee. As Roosevelt read his speech, he threw the finished sheets aside, letting them sail where they would, knowing that the audience would pick them up for souvenirs! He was always an actor!

How far I am ahead of my story! We are not yet out of the covered wagons. It was not long before we were settled, and I began to know all the folks on "the hill," as the neighborhood was called. Elizabeth was soon employed at the hospital as "dining room girl" to the head doctor at Building K. She helped the cook and learned to make a new and wonderful cake called angel food.

Moving into this wooded section of the state was so different than the arid West. Since that was all we children had ever known, things were of great interest to us. For instance, the frequent, gentle rains watering the lush gardens, apples and other fruit hanging from the trees, a neighbor's beehives, walnuts and pecans along the streams, and squirrels barking and jumping from limb to limb in the tall trees. Father said he would take a crack at the squirrels as soon as the season was in. And then the stillness, I think, was the thing that Mother most appreciated; it was so nice to step out and not be whipped to pieces by that everlasting wind.

Father did not like his work at the hospital and soon gave it up to do carpentry work in the large Missouri Pacific Railroad shops downtown. He made more money—fifty cents an hour! It meant carrying his lunch and a mile-and-a-half walk each way.

We stayed in the little house only until fall, when we moved up on the corner into the prettiest house in the settlement. A block away was Wardell's Hotel and Livery Barn. Jo was attracted to the horses and spent all of his spare time there. We knew where to look for him if he was missing!

Next door to us lived a family by the name of O'Brian. The father was one of the bakers at the hospital. There were three girls, one of whom I ran around with, and a little blue-eyed, curly-haired boy named Walter. In a few months, they moved away, and of all of the astonishing coincidences, fifty-one years later, our son-in-law, Dr. Norman Beaty (no near relative) was with Governor Gates en route from Indianapolis to Vincennes as guests on the Freedom Train when the governor introduced Norman to the director: Dr. Walter O'Brian!

"Beaty?" he said. "Should you by any chance be a relative of a girl I used to know by the name of Lida Beaty?"

You can imagine his amazement when Norman said, "Yes, she is my mother-in-law!"

Walter sent me a copy of the official book of the Freedom Train, *Heritage of Freedom*, inscribed as follows:

> For Lida Beaty Jackson. You may not remember the little curly-haired, freckled-faced boy who lived next door at Osawatomie, but I remember you as being my first love. I am that boy. Love and best wishes, Walter H. S. O'Brian, Freedom Train Director, 24 July, 1948"

HIGH SCHOOL

I really dreaded the entrance into high school. It sounded so forbidding. The high school consisted of the upper floor of one small brick building, two rooms, and the office (in which classes were held). There were three teachers. Professor Ewing was sleek, had thin lips, and clipped off his words in a way that made the chills run down your spine—whether you were guilty or not. Never will I forget Miss Sadie Belle Mann's calm, severe, and unsmiling countenance. She was the daughter of the Presbyterian minister. Miss Lila Webber was not long graduated, but she was good-humored and bouncy, looking at us over the tops of her spectacles, invoking mirth that was hard to hide.

Students could choose between two courses: English for two years or Latin covering three. Being a short-cutter, I signed up for the English. It was well enough that I did since a serious illness occurred in my second year, preventing my graduation until the following year.

One Saturday in early September, Father hired a "surrey with the fringe on top" and took Mother and us children to the county fair at Paola, the county seat. All of the displays, shows, and horseracing were great sights for us prairie-grown youngsters. And on the spot, Elizabeth and I had a daguerreotype picture made. As we walked along gaping at the wonders, we came to a booth where folks were inserting a rubber tube in their ears. Then they would wear a look of surprise, laugh, and exclaim with amazement and delight.

"Come right on up, folks, and see and hear for yourselves, the greatest invention of the age, Thomas A. Edison's talking machine!" One of my

THE CRAZY QUILT OF LIFE

precious nickels went to pay for that rare experience, hearing "canned music" for the first time.

The first year of school went well. The next autumn on Thanksgiving, 1898, Elizabeth was married to John H. Burbank, of Miltonvale, Kansas, a man who had come to the institution to work. He was a tall fellow with brown eyes and wavy brown hair. He had been married once before, but his wife had died, leaving a dear little girl named Gracie to live with John's parents in Miltonvale. They were Catholics, but Elizabeth and John were married by the Congregational minister. After a trip to Miltonvale, they went to housekeeping in a little house next to where we had first lived. They were so happy.

Spring came, and we made another move. In mentioning the families on the hill, I omitted the Van Horns. They lived around the corner and owned four or five lots that were in fruit and vegetables. It was across from the Clint Matthews and just back of where we first lived. The house was small, old, and weather-beaten. The fine well, great shade trees, fruit cave, and the fruit trees themselves appealed to Father so much that he traded his wagon and team, which for some reason he had held on to, for the old house and lots. He quit work long enough to add three small rooms, and we moved over.

Six weeks before school was out, I contracted a very severe case of pneumonia. The doctor told me that my determined fight carried me through. I was not conscious of that, however, except when a few young people came in to see me one evening. And being too weak to talk, I smiled at them, closed my eyes, and thought, *They think I'm going to die, but I am not!* I might have, had not Father, on the advice of the doctor, run all of the way to town to get some whiskey, which was administered in small doses when passing through the crisis. I certainly give him and the day-and-night nursing of Mother, who was not well herself, the credit for my being here to tell this tale. During the day, Elizabeth came over. But since she was expecting her baby and was anything but strong, Mother would not have her stay at night. It took me most of the summer to pull out of it. Those were the days before penicillin and vitamins.

It grieves me now—after more than half a century—to have to tell the story of the great tragedy that befell us. On September 29, a baby boy was born, but Elizabeth died on October 4. Those were the days of gross ignorance and carelessness on the part of many doctors; many mothers lost their lives needlessly, and we felt that she had as well. She named her baby David, after Father.

I cannot dwell upon our grief, but it was ever with us since Mother wanted to keep the baby and John assented. She was not well and mourned unceasingly as she cared for him. John bade us a sorrowful farewell and went back to Miltonvale. It was a dreary, lonely winter for her with Father at work and we children at school. However, I would always hurry home to help her all that I could with the washing, ironing, and cleaning. Saturdays were always full days.

There was one girl among my friends who was a comfort to us, and she continued to be my best friend during all the years I lived there. Caddie Barr was so kind and sympathetic, and Mother loved her. How terrible that, within a few years, she and Edna Sleppy should lose their lives in childbirth—each with a different doctor.

Caddie lived in the country and would often come in to spend Saturday nights with us and stay until Monday morning. On Sunday mornings, we would be off to church, attending first one and then another, often going to the home of one of her three sisters who lived in town. After a good dinner, we would stay for evening services. We would walk home, usually in company with a group of other youngsters from the hill who had come down to church.

For some unknown reason—I could not explain it then and am not enough of a psychologist to explain it now—I would not go into the Congregational church with Mother and Elizabeth when we first arrived in Osawatomie. Not that I felt irreligious—I just did not want to. It really must have grieved them both, though I don't recall that they said much to me about my unusual action. One evening, Caddie and I attended the Christian church. Reverend Stottler gave the invitation, and I went forward, united with the church. The next Sunday, I was baptized the way they did it in the Bible—immersed. I had been sprinkled in the Congregational church, and I wonder if my great-great-grandfather (I have found out in my later years that Samuel was a crusader for immersion instead of sprinkling as real baptism) had sent his ideas down along the line to me!

There is a line somewhere among accepted classical observations that suggests that "a divine destiny shapes our ends." However that is, it is quite certain that my joining the Christian church that night very definitely started me along the path where I faced blessings, opportunities, and honors that would never have appeared had I not made that decision. I suppose that everyone, however, could point to some experience in life that was a vital pivot that set his face in a certain direction and led him on to definite accomplishments.

From that day, the church was a very real and tangible part in my life. I became very much interested in Christian Endeavor and sang in the choir. And it was not long until I was teaching a class of boys—Bill among them.

The last semester of school found my work lighter, and I could leave home an hour later, which made my walk coincide with the time that the state hack took the children of the doctors of the institution. Occasionally, if there was room, they would stop and pick me up. I almost envied dainty Esther Van Nuys, who was always bringing flowers to Miss Mann from the big greenhouse of the hospital. Esther's brother was in college, preparing to be a doctor. She and her mother, who often rode with her, spoke so frequently of Walter. Lucky people, I thought, at the top of the ladder. I considered myself most certainly at the bottom.

Twenty years later, when we were living in the governor's residence, Dr. Walter Van Nuys, superintendent of the hospital for the mentally ill at New Castle, invited the governor and me to spend the day and look over the institution. When we arrived, imagine my surprise to find the doctor's houseguest was none other than Esther's mother! She was as much surprised as I was. It had never occurred to me that the family was the same that I had known on "the hill."

GRADUATION AND PIKE'S PEAK

Things began to brighten in the spring; I was graduating. Father gave me five dollars to buy my outfit. Caddie's sister, Anna Bundy, made my white lace-trimmed dress for a dollar and my pink gingham for parties and baccalaureate for fifty cents, leaving me plenty for a pair of shoes!

It has often been remarked that graduation from high school is the greatest thrill of one's life—no matter what may happen afterward. That can well be, at least insofar as a feeling of importance is concerned. I labored for weeks over my essay on "Bread," typifying humanity's effort to make a living, and the dignity of it. It was alive (or maybe dead!) with quotations from Plato to Emerson. To glorify housekeeping, I ended with a flourish:

> *Beauty must come back to the useful arts, and the distinction between the fine and the useful arts be forgotten. For surely there is no better way for woman to serve mankind than by skillful service in the home.*

Emerson must have felt the trembling of the bands of restrictions that bound the women of his time, surmising there was about to be a break.

There were eleven in our class of 1900. Maize (not common yellow) and blue were our class colors, and we chilled the air with our yells, which I secretly thought blunt with no rhythm at all. But it was hard to manage that 1900 business. So it evolved:

THE CRAZY QUILT OF LIFE

> Rah, rah, ree
> Rip, re, roo (long o)
> Osawatomie High School
> Class of double O, See?

We all thought that the "see" at the last was quite cute.

Two nights before graduation, the superintendent, Mr. Ewing, dealt me a fearsome blow. I received a note that ran about like this:

> Having failed in one of your recent examinations, I am asking you to be at my house with paper and pencil at eight o'clock on next Tuesday evening. You need not mention this to anyone, as I shall not.
>
> Sincerely Yours,
> Hue H. Ewing

Needless to say, I didn't mention it. I appeared the next night all set to take that horrid physics examination, knowing full well that I'd never do as well as I had at first, which I felt sure was below passing. I had hoped my daily class grades would carry through. Evidently, they had not!

My heart was heavy as I knocked at the door. When I was invited in, half the class jumped out at me and, with laughter and shouts, pushed me into a side room with them so that we might be ready for the next gloomy one to appear. We had all received the same message! How relieved I was! One of the games that we played at the party was "All's Well That Ends Well."

The graduation was held in the old opera house above the bank on the corner. The class being small, each member had a part in the program. One of the boys spoke on the "Boxer Uprising," another member spoke on "The Sham of Veneer." There were others, then a duet and a solo. The diplomas were presented, and gifts and flowers were sent up to us, some receiving many more than others.

My "Bread" was evidently baked to a turn; the president of the school board made his way up to the platform and giving me a hearty handshake in congratulation said, "Yours was the best of all." That made me happier than if I had carried home an armload of gifts. The article the next week, which appeared in the *Graphic*, the town paper, was very nice indeed, concluding with the idea that I would "have a well-ordered home." Ah! Me! Could he know now that I buy our bread, and it's sliced at that!

Just after graduation, Father asked me to go with him to Colorado on a little train trip to see the mountains and maybe walk up Pike's Peak. Since he worked for the railroad, he could obtain passes. I wanted Mother to go in my stead, but she wouldn't leave the baby with me. I wonder now why they had such a thing in their mind as that trip.

We took a box of food to last until we reached Pueblo. We visited with one of Mother's cousins, Thursa Pumphrey, and then on up to Colorado Springs. When we alighted, Father asked a bystander if he could direct us to a cheap but respectable boardinghouse.

"Come with me to my house," he said.

Entering the little cottage, we found his wife was as hospitable as he had been. Mr. Richardson was as great a talker as Father was. And if you knew Father, you can imagine what went on until late bedtime!

The next morning, we tackled Pike's Peak, following the cog road. That was the most breathtaking (literally) experience I have ever had. It was nine miles up that thing! I stood it well until about the last mile, when I could go only a short distance without stopping to rest. Father and Mr. Richardson seemed not in the least fagged as they plodded on up. Nine-year-old Freddie scampered and capered about like a squirrel, shouting encouragement back to me.

I envied the passengers on the little train as it chugged past us, and yet I would not have exchanged places with them. I was doing a stunt! I had signed my name in a book at the halfway house, along with the others that had walked to the summit!

At each turn on the steep trail, I would say, "Maybe around this curve, it will be more level."

But Freddie would prepare me for the worst by saying, "No, it will be straighter-upper." He was always right!

Along the way, I marveled at the lovely flowers that pushed themselves up between the patches of snow. They must have been anemones. There was a little stream fed by the snows from which we drank as we pulled along. I found a little Pullman-marked tumbler there, which I scrubbed in the crystal water and appropriated for my own use (it now has a Pike's Peak tag and sits in the corner cupboard, waiting to be treasured, I hope, by some of my descendants someday).

At last, the top—the reward that makes it all worth it! It must be a sort of ego that prompts the idea. If it couldn't be told or published, I doubt there would be so many mountain climbers (now that's a cynical comment from a seventy-year-old). I was then eighteen, and it was a challenge. I had climbed my Matterhorn! I've lived to tell it these fifty-two years, though I haven't told it often at that.

It's fun to think of Father and I, prairie folk, up on what seemed the top of the world—a rocky, rugged place, unlovely, in fact, that we had struggled so hard to reach. We might look back down upon the loveliness that we had left behind! It was lovely there in the late evening. The sunset, lights at Cripple Creek, and the brilliant checkerboard suddenly flashed into being over shadowy cities below us: Manitou, Colorado Springs, and adjoining Colorado City.

The summit house provided us with a good snack of sandwiches and coffee. After Father and I had snowballed each other, we began to think of starting back. Picking up an empty flask, which I spotted among the rocks, I filled it with snow to take home as a souvenir. I started off down the track ahead of them. How rested I felt; I thought the return trip was going to be a snap. I was using my "hold-back" muscles instead of my "pull-up" ones! The moon was bright as day, and with the goings easy, we were soon at the timber line. In due time, we were at the halfway house where we submitted proof that we had reached the top. There were our names in the little paper that we proudly brought home as evidence of our mountain lark. By that time my pull-back muscles were groaning under the load, and I told the folks that I thought I would just double up and roll the rest of the way down!

It was some ordeal, and when we finally had made the nine miles down by about four o'clock in the morning, the street cars had quit running. We walked the additional three miles to Colorado City to our rooms! I guess I didn't have to be carried in, but I know you will think I'm telling you the truth when I say that I was in bed all of the next day! Twenty-one miles! That would have been a terrific jaunt on the level with plenty of way stations with food and rest, but up and down that mountain! I was crazy! Father had wanted me to stay at the summit and come back on the cog train, but no—what others had done, I knew I could do. But isn't it a wonder that I have lived to tell this tale?

The trip didn't tell Father anything; after a good breakfast. he and Mr. Richardson set out and explored the Cave of the Winds and other impressive sights. They saved, however, the Garden of the Gods and the gold mill until the next day, hoping that I would be able to accompany them. I was able to and apparently none the worse for having subdued Pike's Peak.

The next day, when we were ready to start home, Mr. Richardson refused to accept anything for our board and room, saying that he had enjoyed Father so much—and he had enjoyed a real vacation himself. Of all the Colorado wonders, that beat them all! Though money was hard to come by for us, Father left a bill in a convenient place for Mrs. Richardson to find after we departed. On our way home, we relived those wonderful days; how I envied the people who lived amidst such scenery.

When I saw Pike's Peak again many years later on our return trip from the governor's conference at Cheyenne, I merely saluted the old wrestler and said, "Remember when?"

THE MOST EXCITING NEWS

Back home again, the summer was before me (and winter too), with no definite plans except a dream that I wanted to go to Kanas University at Lawrence. I sent for information and had some correspondence with the registrar, which added up to the fact that, with no money and no way to get any, it was a hopeless situation. At least I thought it was.

Perhaps with the same determination that I exhibited in walking up and down Pike's Peak, I would have found a way. I was restless and wanted something to happen to show me which way to go. I wouldn't "work out," and all the stores had a full quota of clerks. Of course, I could get work at the asylum. The name of the hospital for the mentally ill had not yet been conceived, but I couldn't bring myself to the place where I thought I could work with those poor, distressed people. Those great brick buildings with the barred windows through which floated the calls of the unhappy patients repelled me.

In the meantime, I was having plenty of fun with a group of young country folks living north of town—Caddie was among them. The young men all had pretty horses and rubber-tired buggies, so picnics, church, or parties at someone's home kept my immediate future planned to the hilt.

Each evening, Joe or I would go to a neighbor's after milk. And on one particular evening when they were having such a grand game of ball, I volunteered to go for them. On the way, I met Father coming home from work,

He stopped just long enough to say, "Hurry back because I have some good news."

When I arrived home to hear the news, Father said, "Well," in the most dramatic way possible (and he could be dramatic), "the school board met last night and elected you to teach the fifth grade!"

At his words, chills hot and cold raced up and down me. I was shocked dumb. Paradise had opened! Of all the experiences of life up to now, that was the most amazing, unexpected, and joyful jolt I had ever had.

"But a certificate—I haven't any," I finally gasped.

"They want you to go the Normal, which starts next week. They gave you the job because they wanted to favor one of their own graduates. And since your high school record was good, they selected you."

It seemed inconceivable to me. And looking back, I think that "Bread" essay had a lot to do with it; the president of the board was a fat man and liked to eat! Who knows?

From that moment, there was plenty of stirring at our house. The Normal was a six-week course for teachers given each summer at Paola, the county seat, six miles distant from our town. Mother made me two or three blouses, and with ribbon bows for my hair and matching ones for my collars, I was all set to go. Friends took me over to find a boarding place.

By the next Monday, I was on hand with notebook and pencils and a feeling of some importance. However, I must say that the feeling of importance dwindled considerably every time I thought of the examinations that would follow the course. Could six weeks of cramming possibly prepare me for it? But I just had to make good. That arithmetic! I was a shark in it up to and including all the double-jointed fractions. But a poor fish in it from there on. Somehow I felt that I would get that inevitable whack on the head at the end and go home crushed. But I kept face front and dug into it.

Imagine my consternation when I walked into my math class to see the president of our board sitting in the visitor's corner! Of course, I thought he came to check up on me, and it would have to be in arithmetic. *The worm is beginning to turn,* I thought. But at the same time, I was hoping against hope that I wouldn't be called upon. That worm didn't turn! You must believe me when I tell you that twice I answered questions and gave definitions where others had failed. You should have seen the proud look on that president's face! My heart thwacked and thwacked for fear I would be asked another that I couldn't answer, but I was spared that and, after class, received commendation aplenty from the visitor. Once more, fortune had favored me.

At the beginning of the sixth week, I said, "How I dread to go back and into those examinations!"

In astonishment, Father replied, "Why, you don't have to take those examinations. I thought I told you that. All that they wanted you to do was just attend the Normal to brush up. They gave you the school because of your high school records."

I've heard many beautiful and eloquent speeches in my time, but that speech was the most beautiful and soul-satisfying I have ever listened to. Would miracles ever cease happening to me?

Thinking back, I'm wondering how they ever managed that certificate business. There were a number of high school graduates teaching, and I presume they were appointed in the same manner that I was. I never asked them. Whether it was fair and square, I don't know, but considering the fact that I looked into seventy-five pairs of eyes in the fifth grade that September morning and had signed up to teach them for the sum of twenty-five dollars per month, I suppose it was fair enough. Yes—twenty-five dollars! The new teachers began at that; each year, the salary was increased $2.50 per month until the maximum of forty dollars was reached. The high school and primary teachers were paid more, however. But that twenty-five dollars to me? I wondered how I would spend all of that.

When it was time to draw my first pay, I went to Wild's store, bought a purse on credit, marched across the street to the bank under the opera house, drew my money, marched back across the street, paid for my purse, and was now "on my own."

The four years that followed were about as uneventful as the lives of most school teachers. They were pleasant ones, however, and I made many good friends among the children and their parents. The beginning was a little hectic. It happened that several of the older boys the year before had just about demoralized things in that grade, running out one teacher, and so worried the one chosen to take her place, that she had resigned rather than to try it for another year. That created the vacancy I stepped into. On my very first morning, the janitor walked in and calmly laid, not one, but a half-dozen or more heavy switches on my desk!

It was then that I understood what one board member meant when he had said, "Stand your ground; you'll have some bad boys, and we'll pay you five dollars extra for every one you thrash!" A dead silence fell over the room, and the children looked frightened. And as my stomach turned over a time or two, I began making as diplomatic a speech as knew how. At the end, I said, "I am sure that we will not need these in this fine group."

I had scarcely finished when a paper wad whizzed past my ear and plastered itself on the blackboard. I scrutinized the faces. There wasn't a guilty one among them, though a tall boy at the back of the room became very much interested in his geography! From time to time, other wads flattened themselves on the blackboard—all of which I ignored.

But when recess time came I said, "All may pass out except Frank. I want to speak with him." When they were safely out, I asked him to come to the desk. He wouldn't talk and was sullen. He was a foot and some taller than I and could have knocked me over with one hand. So finally I said, "Frank, not you or any of the others are going to run me out of this school, so if I have to follow the instructions of the board, I can, though it is a very disagreeable duty." With that, I gave him a whack across the legs as hard as I could.

I think it did not hurt him very much, but he turned white as a sheep, didn't move a muscle, and said, "Miss Beaty, if you will stop, I promise to behave myself."

I stopped with the switch in midair. We talked and made a pact. He kept it to the letter, and I never had a more loyal or lovely student. I shall never forget that tall, blond, blue-eyed boy. I think he felt how utterly distasteful the performance was to me and felt sorry for me!

The next day, in the presence of the children, I put the switches on a shelf in the cloakroom where they rested in peace, having done their full duty, and were used no more. I could fill a book with interesting and delightful experiences from those four years. As I look back, I know that, in my inexperience, my judgments were often faulty, but it was mostly a happy time.

THE CRAZY QUILT OF LIFE

Just before school began, Father bought a little house on the corner of Fourth and Pacific. The price was $1,000. After the down payment, which was made by the sale of the hill property, the balance was paid at $10.25 per month to the building and loan. It was only one square from school. What a joy to have hot lunches—and what a relief it must have been to Mother to be through packing cold ones!

Lida's first fifth grade class. Students were normally older in that grade at the time, since most worked at home on the farms.

SOAP, SPICE, AND MISSIONARIES

Joe moved from Wardell's livery stable on the hill to Ben Morlan's livery stable about four blocks west of us. In fact, those horses held such an attraction for him that school dwindled into insignificance. As a result, he quit at the end of the fourth grade and went to driving for Ben. Kansas school laws must have been pretty lax in those days, especially when it came to certificates and attendance.

Things began to look up for us. We had a pretty home and living seemed less strenuous. I was glad to have a share in carrying the expenses; aside from what cash I could spare, I joined a "Larkin soap and spice club," wherein each member in turn selected a premium. Mine was always for furniture.

More and more, I became interested in the church affairs. One evening, we had a guest speaker, Mrs. Fullen, who had gone down to Puerto Rico at the close of the Spanish-American War to represent our church in the establishment of an orphanage. I was greatly interested in her story; she told of the poverty of the people, their lack of education, and the condition of the children left homeless in the wake of the war. At the close of her talk, I asked her more about the situation there. And seeing my interest, she said that she was looking for a young woman who would go back with her to teach in the orphanage. She asked if I would come. The proposition was too big and too sudden. I had no foundation to stand on since it was the first missionary talk I had ever heard. I was greatly interested, but I suppose my vision and my consecration were too limited. Besides, there were the folks. I would be deserting them when they needed me so much. My answer was no.

By no means was this the end of my interest in Puerto Rico. Through *Missionary Tidings*, I kept in touch with the new mission there and learned that Mrs. Fullen succeeded in securing Miss Nora Siler of Lawrence, Kansas, as the teacher "in my place."

About five years later, when I was married and we had moved to Larned, I joined the little missionary society of half-dozen members. I was soon elected president; I canvassed the church membership for new members and enrolled all of the women except one. Some of the interested husbands joined also; in a year, we were able to support our own missionary on the field with our cash offerings. Who do you suppose we chose? Yes, Miss Nora Siler of Puerto Rico! In two years, she was home on furlough and was a guest in our home. I am positive she was a better teacher than I ever was or could have been, though she may not have been as good at raising funds. So the best plan prevailed.

My interest in worldwide missions has never diminished, and it is directly responsible for my being in Indiana today.

HERBERT PEARCE

In my third year of teaching, a young man named Herbert Pearce came to Osawatomie to work on the town paper. The *Osawatomie Graphic* was owned and edited by Mr. C. C. Clevenger. Probably through the influence of Mrs. Clevenger, who was a member, Mr. Pearce began attending our church. One evening, he came to Christian Endeavor and, as president, I asked our guest to speak. After the meeting, we were introduced by John Slosson, a young printer.

Herbert's said, "I was interested in that definition of 'faith' that you quoted. Where do you find it?"

"It is in Hebrews 11:1," I answered.

He came a few more times to Christian Endeavor; we began having dates, and in a few weeks we were engaged. Since I had contracted to teach the sixth grade the following year, we planned to be married the following June. Hardly had the fall term begun when he was called home by the illness of his father. He remained there to carry on his father's work as editor of the *Aurora Advertiser*.

Perhaps here is the place to set down all that I know of the Pearce family history. Athens, Tennessee, was the home of the Pearces as far back as we now know (it would be a good place to start for some research work). Hamilton Pearce married Caroline. To them, six children were born: John, Allen, Charles, Ellen, another, and Henry Addison in 1849, who became Herbert's father. Herbert's mother was a Scott; of that family, Herbert's grandfather was William Scott, a Civil War soldier, who married Elzira

Johnson, a relative of President Andrew Johnson. They lived in Exeter, Missouri.

Elzira was a heroine. A drunken Negro broke into their house one night when her husband was away. He was about to attack her, but she offered him food to distract him momentarily. Then she slipped behind him and hit him in the head with an ax, killing him on the spot. William and Elzira had nine children; seven of whom were Jane, Mattie, Mary, Rufus, Jerry, Willie, and Edna Josephine, Herbert's mother, who was born April 25, 1854.

Henry and Edna were married in 1871 when she was only seventeen. She was living with her oldest sister Jane, going to school—and Henry was the teacher! She said that she fell in love with him at first sight when he came riding up on a pretty horse to see about getting the job. He was so nicely dressed, and his newly shined shoes just glistened. He really was her Prince Charming. She had always loved him so, and when I came to know her after he was gone, she idolized his memory. He was a fine man, and any descendant of his could think of him with pride. He studied law and was appointed judge in Berryville, Arkansas. All of their four children were born there: Herbert, Horace, Maddie, and Tom. When Herbert was twelve, they moved to Marionville, Missouri, not far from where his father ran a newspaper. Later they went to Billings with another paper. Their last move was to Aurora, at the foot of the Ozarks, where he owned and edited the *Aurora Advertiser*.

What Herbert thought to be a few weeks away from Osawatomie proved to be a permanent move as his father grew steadily worse. And during an operation in the following January, he passed away.

Horace, now a Christian Disciples minister, married Myrtle Seamens, a primary schoolteacher in Mount Vernon, a nearby town where he had his first pastorate.

Maddie also was married that spring to Gordon Emmons, a handsome and pleasant person, coming from one of Aurora's best families; his father was a former mayor. They lived with her mother for a few months while remodeling their home a few doors away. Tom, with the merry brown eyes, was seventeen, bright as a tack, but they all loved to tease him.

In the meantime, Herbert began building our little cottage just two squares away from his mother's house. Three rooms and a bath, the fixtures in the latter room were to be added when we were able. A barn was being built to shelter our lady, the little bay that was to take us riding in the red-wheeled buggy over those beautiful Ozark trails. Rain hindered the work on the house so much that, one day in May, I received a letter that said, "I have decided that we better postpone our wedding for a month." What a disappointment! There was just no romance in a July wedding! I soon became reconciled, however, since it would give me time to finish several embroidery pieces that I had begun. And the letters were now coming thick and fast.

The morning of July 19, 1904, eventually dawned. Caddie had stayed all night with me since we had to rise rather early to be ready for the ceremony by nine o'clock. We were to take a train at Paola around noon that would take us home. Things began to stir. We had a hurried breakfast, and while Caddie and I did the dishes, Mother arranged bouquets of pink rose of Sharon in the living room and dining room, along with the sweet-scented bergamot that she loved so much. Mrs. Salsbury, a neighbor, sent a large bouquet of Cecile Brunner roses. They were the ones from which Mother started plants from, which we all have bushes. Also, the roses were the ones that Jo and Margaret wore in their wedding bouquets, as I did. I suppose that Ann and Caroline will also have a bud or so tucked in their bouquets.

The time had come to dress for that long-awaited moment. Herbert had said once that he didn't care what kind of a dress I wore—just as long as it wasn't white. I selected a very tiny checked blue foulard, made tight-waist, of course, and sweeping the floor. The full-elbow sleeves were finished with a four-inch lace ruffle, and the wide, pointed collar falling over the shoulders was bordered with white embroidered applique. The applique followed the seam of the sides of the front panel. The other wide gores of the skirt were shirred to fit the hips. Want to see it? It's right there in the closet, done up in tissue paper. It will soon be fifty years old. A black skirt, white lace-trimmed blouse, and a full-sleeved black taffeta jacket was my traveling outfit. My trunk was packed with my treasures—quilts and linens, so many nice ones from the shower that the girls gave me. Dishes, pictures, bisque vases from Bill, silver sugar and creamer spoon holder set from Joe, Havilland plates and so many loving gifts from Mother and Father in the months past—little things that I had added to my store and gloated over.

Herbert had come in the evening before, bringing Horace along to perform the ceremony. They spent the night with the Clevengers. And as I had Caddie do the final hooking-up on my tight waist, I kept peeking out the west window for a glimpse of the bridegroom.

The preacher and the bridegroom arrived on time, and—before you could shake a stick—I was Mrs. Herbert Bancroft Pearce! Nine o'clock in the morning is a most unromantic time to have a wedding. It is too late for a breakfast, according to our standards, and too early for lunch. Nevertheless, Mother said we must have something to eat. So, on the day before, I had baked a chocolate cake; while we were finishing, Father slipped out and walked in with the hugest watermelon that I have ever seen before or since! It was his contribution to the festivities.

Somehow, I didn't feel so festive. I knew what my leaving meant to the folks. Brave and jolly good-byes were said as we climbed into the surrey with Horace, John, and Caddie and started for Paola. A block away, I discovered that I had left my silk jacket; upon returning for it, I found Mother in tears. I would not be home often—and I know now how they felt with Margaret in Wisconsin and Joe in Oklahoma. She often used to say, "If you just live near so you could run in often, how wonderful it would be!"

Though I do have many sharp moments of longing, I have a notion that separation is best in many ways, particularly as far as children are concerned. There is a minimum of interference in their family life, and the parents just have to find new interests that call them out of themselves into useful activities of one kind or another.

LARNED

Was I ever surprised when Horace came over from Mount Vernon to tell us he had accepted a call to the Christian church in Larned, Kansas. Of all places, out in the "short-grass" country and just a few miles east of our stamping ground, Jetmore. I turned loose and told him all about the country and how very different they would find it from the calm wooded section in which we lived. High winds, dust storms days on end, and often drought during the late summer, but in July everything and everybody seemed to enveloped in the great golden wheat harvest. Planted in the fall, it grew and ripened and was put away before the dry, blistering days of summer.

In a week, they were packed and gone, but not without a farewell supper at our house. Mother Pearce was sad at their leaving for such a distant home, knowing that she would seldom see them and their little Leroy. Tom went west to Oregon with his cousin, Garfield Stubblefield, a surveyor to work in the reclamation service. I cannot recall whether he left before or after her death. He is still there at Grant's Pass and is the water commissioner for the district.

The next thing that happened was a letter from Horace telling Herbert that there was a good opening for him as business manager of the county paper, *The Tiller and Toiler,* if he would agree to come immediately. Now that was the bombshell! Mother Pearce had some time since they had sold *The Advertiser,* and Herbert was running a job printing office. He had plenty of work, but the low prices paid none too well; a good salary and coming in regularly was a great temptation. We fell for it, sold our house to Gordon and Mattie, and were gone. I was headed once more to western Kansas! It would be interesting to know how many families have changed their location by answering a relative saying, "Come on in—the water is fine!" And how many have been good swimmers, and how many have sunk! Well, we didn't sink. It was a good move for us, as we could see then and for several years afterward.

In the spring of 1907, Myrtle and Fred Sweet lived at Pierce City, just a few miles from us. They decided to go back to Kansas with us and go into the carpentry business at Larned. Both families moved into a big rambling one-story, white house until Fred could build our cottage, which we lived in but a short time, having a chance to sell at a good profit. We rented a nice house on State Street.

Herbert liked his new work. He liked Mr. Harvey Eckert, the editor and publisher of *The Tiller and Toiler*, and people liked him. Herbert carried a dignity that commanded the deepest respect of everyone, and yet he was so kind and gracious that he drew people to him and won their confidence. He was a good planner and immediately put in motion his ideas for increasing the subscription and enlarging the number of advertisers. Mr. Eckert was a cripple and very often quite ill; it was a great pleasure for him to see Herbert's quick appraisal of situations and his correct handling of them. He soon became acquainted with businessmen and farmers all over the county.

Of course, we entered the church the first Sunday that we were there—and I was soon up to my neck in its activities. I taught a class of teenage girls and sang in the choir. I asked about the missionary society and was told that there were a few that met with the aid society; about all they did was pay their dues. I found them, over in one corner, not over a half-dozen members paying their fifteen cents per month and talking over a little business. I startled them by asking if they would like to have a new member. Of course! From then on, I began to work in a larger way in the missionary field.

Though there was still a great deal of prejudice regarding the missionary program, particularly involving foreign missions, in the church, I saw a field as ripe to harvest as the numberless acres of wheat nearby. Accordingly, I asked them to meet with me for the next meeting. At the same time, I asked the ladies on the other side of the room to come since the date would not conflict with aid day.

Many came—and also others who I had invited during the month intervening. I was asked by the president to make a talk. I made a little one setting forth the cultural and broadening effects of the study of world missions as well as the spiritual needs of it. More than a dozen women enrolled as new members. I served angel food cake after an Aurora recipe, and I can't remember what else. But the dear old lady who was president was so overjoyed with the success of the meeting that she asked me to serve as chairman of the program committee.

From then on, the meetings were held in the homes and always with a social hour following, during which members were being continually added. Though we followed the programs as outlined in *Missionary Tidings*, our national magazine, I introduced many novel ideas and features that were not only entertaining but that gave each member a definite part in the program. This resulted in the ever-widening horizon of world missions for the entire group.

While on this subject I will continue to discuss my work in this activity while in Larned, since it had a very definite bearing upon future events in my life. It was not long before I was elected president of the society, and I set about to enlist every woman in the church as a member—the requirements were the payment of fifteen cents per month with optional "special" offerings. We succeeded in this effort—with the exception of one woman who was afraid of her husband! He forbade her to join. This was more than made up by the names of several men that we enrolled.

We made our programs as colorful as possible, using native costumes, foods peculiar to the countries studied, and wall decorations (we had outgrown the living rooms and met in a large classroom in the basement of the church). Maps and charts and pictures gave the room an air of a classroom—and it really was. Contributions were made to provide a library of a few good missionary books, and each group leader (there were twelve groups) saw to it that her group read its full quota each month.

During a visitation for new members, I called upon a dressmaker out at the edge of town. As I explained the nature of our work, she was unusually interested and seemed delighted to become a member. Mrs.

Bertha Snyder became a fast friend, and her enthusiasm for the work could not have been exceded. And not only that, she was very capable and was always at my side to help put over any program or project. Not only did the local work interest us, but she and I attended the district and state conventions as well, from which we returned bubbling over with new aims to be accomplished.

Mrs. Josephine MacDaniel (later Stearns), a returned missionary from Mexico, was our state secretary. She was a stately, beautiful woman and an eloquent speaker. We heard her at the state church convention at Topeka, and I remarked that if we could induce her to come to Larned for an address—since our church had become so missionary-conscious—I believed we could become a "Living Link Church." We asked her, and she said that she would come for our "Woman's Day," which in all of our churches is still the first Sunday in December. We went home walking on air, and I doubt there was the slightest hesitation in our minds that we would fail in our undertaking.

We took the good news to our pastor, Reverend MacCrae (Scotch)—Horace had long since gone—and he said we could never do it and shouldn't attempt it! There is something in the Kansas air that tells you with every breath you breathe that you can do the well-nigh impossible if you'll just take another breath. Well, after the pastor pronounced his verdict, we each took another breath and very respectfully said, "We think we can do it."

Maybe Presbyterians, Lutherans, and Congregationalists are wondering what a Living Link Church is. That is a church that supports its own missionary on the field. In that day, it was $600. We had a church membership of between 300 and 350, so that amount had to be raised aside from offerings to other missions and benevolences—to say nothing of the regular expenses of running the church. I'll now admit that it did seem rather lofty. Young people rule as if mountain climbing. Therefore, with our eyes upon the "summit," we set out to obtain as many pledges as possible. These were to be paid quarterly—before the day when our guest speaker would arrive. I am sure that God had a hand in that effort; by the time that our Woman's Day rolled around, almost the entire amount had been pledged and much of it paid. The offering that night enabled us to set our pennant upon the mountaintop! Would you guess who we chose as our Linking Link? It was none other than Miss Nora Siler of Puerto Rico!

That night, we entertained Mrs. MacDaniel in our home and rejoiced over our great accomplishment. Larned continued to be a Living Link church—and it still is—though Miss Siler has long since retired. Mrs. MacDaniel, later as Mrs. Stearns, often stopped at our home when in our part of the state and frequently invited me to accompany her on her visits to the churches. Occasionally, I was asked to speak at the state conventions in our round-table sessions—and once on the regular all-church program when the state convention was held at Parsons.

In a few years, the national secretary of the Christian Women's Board of Missions in Indianapolis passed on, and Mrs. Stearns was called to headquarters to take her place.

It may sounds like it, but by no means did I spend all of my time in church activities. Herbert and I had many friends in town and the country where we visited. I sewed a great deal, making all of my housedresses and Herbert's shirts! I had no electric sweeper, washer, or refrigerator, but with room, tub, washboard, icebox, and the other "non-labor-saving" devices, I "kept house" as well as the average, I suppose.

We lived in a pretty house on State Street. But it was not long before the owners had made so much money on wheat that they wanted to move into town to take it easy. I had just hung the last curtain, which wound up my spring housecleaning when they broke the news! For a few hours, it broke my heart, but it was quickly healed when Herbert came home and said that, since we were paying all that rent, we had better be applying it to our own home. We would build us another one out by the city standpipe where lots were reasonable; on the hill, we would have a fine view of the Arkansas River Valley.

While building our little cottage, we lived in a house nearby and I watched it grow every day. When the high and often hot and dusty wind of the day had lulled itself into a dreamy breeze for the night, we would stroll over to the house to see what the workmen had accomplished. Fred and Myrtle had long since returned to their former home at Jetmore, so the work was being done by two local young men who had just hung out their shingles as contractors.

Not only did we have a new house—we had a new barn as well! I had the loveliest and liveliest black driving horse you can ever imagine hitched to a top buggy. Herbert gave her to me for my birthday. She shone like satin and had the high spirit of a thoroughbred, arching her neck and prancing when I drove downtown just as if she was in a show ring. She really tried to show off, which is a trick I suppose her former owner had taught her. I had to hold on to those reins. People said that she would someday tear the buggy into splinters and finish me off at the same time, but I was not afraid of that. I sensed that she knew exactly what she was doing.

And one day, I was quite justified in thinking that very thing. It happened at the county fair one morning when I had taken a loaf of salt-rising bread to exhibit. She had pranced and sidestepped as I had driven her in and out among the buggies, wagons, and a few automobiles, but she stood quietly without hitching at the entrance of the women's booth while I registered and made my entry. I hopped in the buggy and had gone only a short distance toward the gate when, as she was doing some fancy didoes, a strap on her bridle broke. She stopped as the bridle fell from her head onto her shoulders. I saw at once I couldn't fix it—and she didn't wait for me to try. She walked like an old plow horse through that gate and headed for home as straight as an arrow. With her head free and my guiding her by very gentle pulls on the reins from her shoulders, she walked sedately to her barn door—like the thoroughbred she was! Did I love that horse! Black Beauty was her name.

In 1911, Edmond M. Madison, congressman from the "Big Seventh" District, died. By special election, a successor would be chosen on the following January 1. George A. Neeley, a young lawyer from Hutchinson, entered the contest on the Democratic ticket. *The Tiller and Toiler*, being a Democratic paper, was of course for him. Herbert was soon up to his ears in plans to further his candidacy. When Neeley dropped into the office one day, he was delighted with the work that had been done. He told Herbert that if he was elected, he would appoint him as his private secretary in Washington. What big news Herbert had to tell me that evening at the supper table! When we finally got down to earth after being in the clouds for a few hours at the mere possibility of going to Washington, every sentence we uttered from then on began with "if."

Herbert worked through the paper and all over the district and was busy every minute. It was in the autumn that all this happened, and I was busy as a beaver myself getting a special program ready for our Woman's Day and helping my class of girls with their Thanksgiving bazaar. Good thing we were busy!

ON TO WASHINGTON

Soon after, Mr. Neeley was elected! Now all of our sentences began with how, when, where, and what. I do not recall just when we were to be in Washington, but I know that we lost no time getting ready.

I think that my first question must have been: "What will we do with Black Beauty?" I knew what the answer was because a man had been trying to buy her. Herbert called him from the office and named the price—and the buyer came out immediately for her. I cannot recall the exact amount, but he had the check all written out and handed it to me.

I looked it over and said, "She is my horse, and you will have to add just fifty dollars to that or you can't have her."

He gave me the fifty in cash, and I had a real surprise for H. B. when he came that evening! I would really have grieved for her had we not such a wonderful adventure before us. Mrs. Snyder made me some lovely dresses (in those days, ready-made dresses were very poorly made and therefore taboo if one wanted something nice). With my Black Beauty money, I was able to outfit myself besides luggage and still had a nice sum in reserve.

About a week before we were to start, I came down with a heavy cold and fever. For a day, the doctor thought I was going to have pneumonia. You can imagine how miserable and unhappy I was. After all these years, I remember the exact words of the doctor when he examined me the next morning.

"You have no pneumonia going or coming!"

With that verdict and plenty of determination, I was able to board the train on the appointed day. We had allowed a day or two extra so that we might go by Osawatomie to see the folks. Herbert had written them that, since I had a bad cold, we might come in a little later. When we arrived on time, the folks were delighted that I had been able to make it. Knowing as they did how long it always takes me to recover from a cold, they were ready to supplement any remedies that I might have along with me. Mother had made me a red flannel, all-wool petticoat and had trimmed it with knitted red yarn lace, which I know had kept her busy many a long evening hour. Father had ready a bottle of cod liver oil! Bless their dear hearts! Dutifully, I donned the petticoat underneath my muslin white one, but that cod liver oil was another story. Father lost his patience with me, and I finally managed to get a dose down. I obediently tucked the bottle into my grip as we said our good-byes.

Sometimes one tragedy will avert another. Upon reaching St. Louis, where we were to change trains, I opened my grip for something in the waiting room. To my horror, all of the little toiletries and necessities I had packed for use on the trip were soaked or swimming in cod liver oil! A tragedy all right, but my dismay was mixed with a deep relief that I was spared the "tragedy" of having to take the stuff. The bottle had come uncorked, and every last drop had escaped. The station attendant, kind soul that she was, washed out my things while I endeavored to wash out my lovely new leather bag of which I was so proud! Apparently, I had it cleaned and dried out by the time the attendant brought me the articles she had dried on a radiator. It was a sorry experience indeed; as we boarded our train, I was relieved and happy that it was over and behind me. It was behind me all right—as far as the mopping up was concerned. But the next time that I opened that grip, it smelled like a fish wharf! And always did! I left it in Washington; if it is still in existence, I'm sure it still does reek of a foul odor.

We were snoozing in our berth early the next morning when our heads collided with the headboard. Somebody said that we had hit a cow, but with that terrific a jar, we thought it must have been something more than a cow. As soon as it was light, the passengers began poking our heads out to see why it had taken them so long to get a dead cow off the track.

We were in the West Virginia mountains and were making a very beautiful and graceful curve around one of them when the "cow" (in the form of a huge boulder) had strayed on the track. The engine had hit "her" center. The boulder didn't budge, but the engine and the baggage car did. They were motionless on their sides—dead as heck. We waited hours for a relief train to pick us up, and we finally reached our destination.

I will not attempt to relate all that we did and all that we saw during those five wonderful months in Washington. W secured a room at 514 East Capitol with Mrs. Thomas Carroll and took our meals with a Mrs. Holland nearby. It was a lovely old street with great trees arching over—and it was just five blocks east of the Capitol.

Since Herbert's work was in the House Office Building, which is adjacent to the Capitol, it was just a nice walk. He did not come back for lunch, so I had the days to myself with nothing to do except to go sightseeing—and I did that with all of the energy and understanding I had. Since I was a history fan (and still am), I gloated over the statues and landmarks on every side—as multitudinous as the soldiers in Washington's army camped here.

At night, I would be dog tired; my poor feet rebelled against such foolishness. But the next day out, I went to stand upon some other spot of "sacred" ground or to tramp through miles of museum aisles. What an experience! I kept a sort of a diary, illustrating it with penny postcards. On weekends, we would go with another couple, a senator's secretary and his wife from the state of Washington, to Rock Creek Park or to some scenic attraction nearby. One trip was to Niagara Falls, and another was to Mount Vernon.

Nearly every day, there was some interesting or notable event that occurred. Once I noted that Clara Barton had died, so I decided that I would go out to the funeral—or rather out to the lovely wooded suburb in which she lived—so that I might view the great procession. It was a surprise to see a mere handful of cars following the remains of the great Clara Barton, founder of the Red Cross. I learned that Washington was "fed up with greats." They were the common run, and if a senator wanted to be great to the point of receiving homage, he had better stay at home in his own district! People move in and out among the shadows of the truly great of the past, and only the newcomer or the tourist stands in reverence and meditation.

LIDA BEATY-JACKSON

We stood in the rain to watch the procession bearing the flag-draped coffins of the soldiers and sailors who had gone down with the *Maine* in Havana Harbor, having been lifted from their watery graves after all these years to take their places amid the long rows of heroes in Arlington Cemetery. Many people lined the streets—some with bowed heads and tear-filled eyes. Later we went out to Arlington to see the sacred cemetery. On either side of the endless aisles were the gravestones of young boys—teenagers and those in their early twenties.

Angry men, too impatient to work out their differences, hurl their beloved children to death on the battlefields! I wonder if it will ever be different (we are currently in the third year of the Korean War with more than 112,000 of Americans alone, dead, wounded, or missing—and with no end in sight, 1952).

We attended the Ninth Street Christian Church. A friend asked if I would like to borrow one of her children so that I might go to the egg-rolling on the White House lawn. I went and was duly admitted at the gate with my "child," who rolled his colored eggs down the slopes and ran after them.

After a time, Mrs. Taft, wife of the president, came out and made small talk with the children. This was a regular custom at Easter. I thought it more sacred ground where great men and lovely women had walked—but none too sacred for little children to frolic upon.

A world-shaking event occurred while we were there: the sinking of the *Titanic* on her maiden voyage. She hit an iceberg, and hundreds of people perished—many Washingtonians among them. Newsboys with extras were all over the place, and excitement ran high. The *Titanic* had been heralded as the greatest boat afloat and practically unsinkable!

Occasionally we went to the theatre. One night, we saw Maude Adams in *Chanticleer*. Another evening, Mrs. Carroll and I went to see *Madame X*—and we wept during most of the performance! The only thing that relieved the tension was a large fat man just in front of us who shook with sobs and blew his nose loud enough to drown out the players! As we went down the street and sat at a refreshment table, we viewed each other's red noses and had a big laugh.

"What a good time we have had," said Mrs. Carroll.

Spring advanced to summer and the session would soon be over. Though we had been to Mount Vernon, I wanted to go again—partly because of Mrs. Carroll. She had lived there for sixteen years and had never been! I told her that she was disgraced—and that I didn't want to leave until she had redeemed herself. One day, we packed our lunch and alighted down the Potomac with a boatload of others to the priceless old mansion. We had a lovely day. When walking through the garden, we came upon the stump of a cherry tree with a sprout beside it bearing cherries. She remarked that we were in the right place; there was the tree that George had cut down! Aside from the more sober moments when we viewed the treasured articles and more sacred spots, the day was filled with lighthearted talk and relaxation. It was climaxed by Margaret's announcement that she was coming to live with us. Mrs. Carroll was the first to hear the joyful news. Next to that, the happiest day in Washington for me was when we left the hot, sultry city and were bound for our breezy Kansas home.

Friends showered me with gifts, and others came out for a nice visit. We had such a good time, though the dry, hot winds reminded her too much of life in the soddy for her to rave about the climate!

I was well; about all we could talk about was the blessed event. Herbert called her "little Lida Jr.," but I called her Margaret. On February 10, 1913, Margaret Lida came to us as a lovely and healthy baby. Dr. C. C. Coons attended us with Miss Reta Gibbs, the only trained nurse in the county. My dear schoolmate and friend, Myrta Sweet, kept the household going until I was up and able to get someone to take over for a while.

She was such a cute baby—and such a good baby. The nearest neighbor once asked if she had ever cried! It was unspeakable joy to have a baby in the house after having gone nearly nine years without one!

But we had a problem to solve. Should we take her to Washington for the next session—or should I remain at home where we thought I could take better care of her? We made a foolish decision as I see it now—Herbert went on alone. He was so lonely without us, and we stayed at home and were so lonely without him.

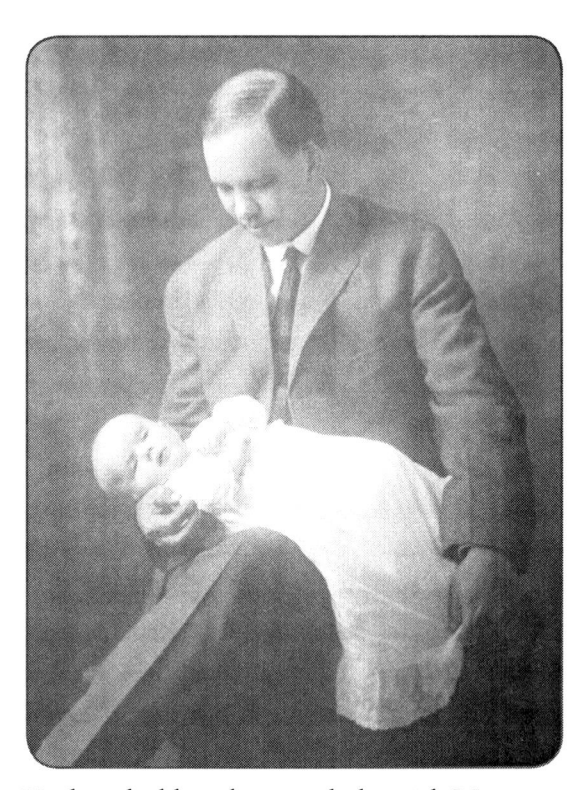

Herbert holding his new baby girl, Margaret

A FAREWELL

From the earliest records, it appears that the compelling urge of all of all these ancestral families was to go west and ever west in search of land. The earliest, and others like them, set out to sea, bound for a strange country that promised not only freedom from political, religious, or economic pressure, but land, much land that would provide adequate room for them and their growing families.

Strictly speaking, we come from an agricultural people, landowners, and lovers of the soil. So those who feel an urge to make a garden, go for it—it is in your blood! Live up to the legacy of your ancestors and make them proud. No finer heritage could we have as sons and daughters of those pioneers.

Lida's father and his great-grandson, Bobby Burbank.
Lida's father was known for his courage,
discipline, intelligence, and joy.

EPILOGUE

Lida and Herbert's baby, Margaret (little Lida Jr.), grew up to be a beautiful young woman. Tragically, Herbert died of diabetes in 1916 when she was only two years of age. Margaret always said that she wishes she could have been a little older to at least have a memory of him.

About six years later, Lida remarried the man who lived next door. Her new husband's name was Edward Jackson. He was an attorney who became the governor of Indiana in 1924.

Margaret went to Indiana University and majored in education. She met my father there, Earl Parker, who became a very successful research chemist. I, Margaret Ann Parker, was born to Margaret Sr. and Earl in 1948. It has been a longtime goal of mine to publish my grandmother Lida's story—and now this goal has been accomplished.

EXTRA STORIES ABOUT LIDA ANN'S ANCESTORS

James Alley—Lida's great-great-great-grandfather
Samuel Alley—Son of James, Lida's great-great-grandfather
Cyrus—Son of Samuel, Lida's great-grandfather
Charity—Wife of Cyrus, Lida's great-grandmother

REVOLUTIONARY WAR TIMES

Records show that James Alley Sr. made settlement in what is now known as Scott County, Virginia, in 1776. It was near Moore's Fort on the headwaters of the Clinch River that they built their cabin. We can imagine that it did not take long for James and his bunch of husky sons to put up that cabin.

Daniel Boone and his family recently had lived in the same settlement, having just a year before gone on to Kentucky. Boone claimed that his wife was the first white woman to stand on the banks of the Kentucky River. Boone had settled on the Clinch for a few years because of the murder of his son James by the Indians. He had been placed in command of the various forts up and down the Clinch and was in direct command of Moore's Fort, "to which his family repaired when faring an Indian attack."

The hearts of Samuel and his brothers must have pounded as they listened to the tales of recent Indian attacks on the settlers and how

THE CRAZY QUILT OF LIFE

they had been repulsed by Daniel Boone and his men. They knew that the silent, sneaking Indian was still nearby—and that he might appear with his scalping knife at any moment, even before the cabin was completed! How my great-great-great grandmother must have feared for her boys in their teens. Indeed, she had reason; the very next year—and a month before he was sixteen—Samuel became an enlisted Indian fighter!

His Revolutionary War record says, "While a resident of Washington County, Virginia, Samuel Alley enlisted in May 1777 and served four months as a private under Captains McLanahan and Snoddy in the Virginia troops, engaging against the Indians at Moore's Fort."

Picture all of the women and children of the settlement rushing into the fort as the men and boys hurried to snatch up their rifles to defend it. The women were molding bullets and reloading the rifles as they were emptied—and our little fifteen-year-old great-great-grandfather right in the midst of it. Perhaps some of his brothers were killed or wounded; we do not know. But it is quite certain that two of his sisters fell into Indian hands. In Robert Addington's *History of Scott County*, he quotes from Sam Alley: "Mrs. Fanny Napper, whose maiden name was Alley, and her five children were killed and scalped near Fort Blackmore in 1777." This fort was a few miles down the Clinch from Moore's Fort.

Since Addington says that James Alley Sr. was the only Alley to take up settlement in the Clinch Valley, it is reasonable to believe that Fanny and Polly of the following story were children of James Sr. and sisters of Samuel. Small wonder that he took up arms! I will copy the story as it appears in Addington's book. No doubt this story, like many others, has had numerous details added in the telling. But each time that it has appeared in stories written of that time, the essentials are the same.

For 150 years, the following most popular and best known traditional story has been told around the Scott County firesides. I quote the story in full from Coale's *Life of Wilburn Waters*, written by Mr. Addington:

> During the spring of 1777, a party of Indians under the lead of the half-breed Benge and a savage white man by the

name of Hargus crossed the range of hills north of Clinch at High Knob and made their way to Ft. Blackmore on Stony Creek (which was not far from what is now known as Osborn's Ford in Scott County). The white man Hargus had been living in the neighborhood but had absconded to the Indians to evade punishment for crime. And he became an inhuman persecutor of his race.

The Indian, having cautiously and stealthily approached the river down Stony Creek, crossed some distance below and came up in the rear of a high cliff south of, and opposite the fort, concealing their main body in the bushes at the base. In order to command a view of the fort, they sent one of their numbers to the summit of the cliff to spy out the condition of the fort and to act as a decoy. He ascended in the night and climbed a tall cedar with foliage at the top, on the very verge of the precipice. And just at the break of day he began to gobble like a wild turkey. This imitation was so well executed it would have been successful but for the warning of an old Indian fighter present by the name of Matthew Grey. Hearing what they supposed to be a turkey and desiring him for breakfast, some of the younger members of the company proposed to go up the cliff and shoot him, but Grey told them if they wanted to keep their scalps on their heads they had better let that turkey alone. And if they would follow his directions he would give them an Indian for breakfast.

Having promised to obey his instructions, he took several of them with him to a branch which he knew to be in full view of the Indians. Then Grey told them to wash and dabble in the stream to divert the attention of the enemy for half an hour while he went to look for the turkey, which still continued to gobble at intervals. Grey, having borrowed an extra rifle from David Cox, crouched below the bank of the stream and in this manner followed its

THE CRAZY QUILT OF LIFE

course to where it emptied into the river, half a mile below to a place known as Shallow Shoals. Here he took to the timber, eluding the vigilance of the Indians by getting in their rear. He then crept cautiously up the ridge, guided by the gobbling of the Indian in the top of the cedar on the cliff.

Getting within about seventy-five yards of the tree and waiting until his turkey ship had finished an extra big gobble, Grey drew a bead upon him and put a ball in his head. With a yelp and a spring the Indian went crashing through the treetops and over the precipice—a mangled mass of flesh and bones. Immediately, a race for life commenced. Grey had played a deeper game and nothing but his fleetness and knowledge of savage craft could save him. He knew that the Indians in ambush would go to their companion on hearing the report of the rifle and that they were not more than two hundred yards away. He did his best running and dodging, but they were so close upon him that he would have been captured or killed, had not the men of the fort rushed out to the rescue.

The Indians started in the direction of Moore's Fort after finding that they had been discovered and that they were not strong enough attack or besiege the fort. The persons at Fort Blackmore, knowing that the settlers at Moore's Fort were not aware that the Indians were in the vicinity, determined to warn them. But the difficulty was how this was to be done and who would be bold enough to undertake the task, as the Indians were between the two forts. When a volunteer for the perilous expedition was called for, Matthew Grey, who but an hour before had made such a narrow escape, boldly offered his services. And getting the fastest horse and two rifles, he started out through the almost unbroken forest. Moving cautiously along the trail, he came near Ivy Spring (about two miles from the fort) and saw signs which satisfied him—that the Indians had halted at the springs. There was no way to flank them, and he must make a perilous dash or fail in his errand of mercy. Seeing an old Indian fighter, he knew that they seldom put out pickets. The trail made a short curve near the spring and he at once formed the plan of riding quietly up to the curve and then, with a shot and a yell, to dash through them.

This he did, and before they had sufficiently recovered from their surprise to give him a parting volley, Grey was out of their reach. He arrived at the settlement in safety, and thus in all probability saved the lives of all the settlers. The Indians, however, captured two women on the way—Polly Alley at Osborne's Ford and Jane Whitaker from up the river.

Finding the fort fully prepared for their reception, the band had to pass on with their captives without permitting them to be seen. Reaching Guess Station, they remained part of the night; finding it well prepared for defense, they continued their journey to the "Breaks," where the Russell and Pound forks of Big Sandy pass through the Cumberland Mountain. After this they traveled every day, resting at night, until they reached the Ohio at the mouth of the Sandy. Crossing the river on raft of logs with their prisoners, who suffered more than can be described or conceived on the long march, they reached their destination at Sandusky. The women were closely confined for some time after, though they were eventually stripped, painted, and allowed the liberty of the village, closely watched for a month or more. But seeing they made no attempt to escape, the Indians abated their vigilance. Observing this, the girls determined to make an effort to escape. Having been permitted to wander about at pleasure from time to time and punctually returning at night, the Indians were thrown off their guard. Having wandered one day farther from the village than usual and being in a dense forest, they started out on their long journey toward home. After traveling all night, they found themselves only about eight miles from the village, and finding a hollow log, they crept into it with the determination of remaining concealed through the day. They had been in it but a few minutes before Hargus and two or three Indians came along in pursuit and sat down upon it. The girls heard them form their plans for the next day's search. Returning late in the afternoon having lost the trail, the Indians sat down upon the same log to rest and again the occupants beneath them heard their plans for pursuit. These were that a party should pass down each of the two rivers which had their sources near their village and emptied into the Ohio. They became very much enraged at having been baffled by two inexperienced girls and threatened their victims with all sorts of tortures should they be recaptured. Hargus, more furious than the Indians themselves was striking his tomahawk into the log to emphasize his threats, and finding it to return a hollow sound, declared the girls might be in it, as they had been traced thus far where the trail was lost and sent one of the savages to the end of the log to see. The savage went and looked but seeing that a spider had stretched its web across the aperture he made no further examination. This web saved them from recapture and possibly from cruel death.

After the Indians left, the girls, having heard their plans, left the log and resumed their weary journey, taking a leading ridge which ran at right angles with the Ohio and led them to it not far from opposite the mouth of the Sandy. They could hear the yells of the men in pursuit each day and night until they reached the river when, from a high promontory, they had the satisfaction of seeing their pursuers give up the chase and turn back toward their village. They had nothing to eat for three long days and nights but a partially devoured squirrel from which they had frightened a hawk.

On the night of the third day after the Indians had relinquished the pursuit they ventured to the river where they were fortunate enough the next day to see a flat-boat with white men in it descending the stream who, on being hailed, took them aboard, set them across at the mouth of Sandy and furnished them with sufficient bread and dried venison to last the two weeks and a blanket each in which time they expected to make their way back to one of the settlements on the Clinch. They took their course up Sandy on the same trail they had gone down some months before, but in one of the rapid and dangerous crossings of that stream, they lost all of their provisions as well as the blankets. This, though a great calamity, did not discourage them, but instead motivated them with the thought of home and loved ones near. They found their way through Pound Gap and reached Guess Station about the middle of September, having been on the journey about a month, all the while encountering hardships and dangers under which many of the sterner sex of the present day would give way.

Those were troubled years. Indian forays were frequent. Men were killed in the fields, and accounts are given where whole families were murdered and scalped. Many were captured and carried into captivity. The Revolution was being fought in the East, and the Indians were encouraged in their depredation in the West.

During 1778, there seemed to be no nearby disturbances. But in June of the next year, the Indians were dangerously near again, which accounts for the next section in Samuel's Revolutionary War record.

"He enlisted June 1, 1779, and served one month as private in Captain Alexander Ritchie's Virginia Company, engaged against the Indians in Powell's Valley. Powell's Valley was just inside the Cumberland Gap."

Two years after Samuel's last encounter, James Sr. came into his own. From records, the historian writes, "On August 23, 1781, 400 acres were surveyed to him on the Clinch River. On November 16, 230 more acres were surveyed to him on the south side of the Clinch River."

THE CRAZY QUILT OF LIFE

That was 630 acres of rich valley land! Our ancestor had become quite the landholder, but he had paid a great price in peril and loss of life. However, it is of such circumstances that pioneers are made.

Though that same fall Cornwallis had surrendered at Yorktown, it did not mean that the British-hired Indians had laid down the arms that England had supplied them via Detroit. Large bands of them were menacing the very existence of the new settlements that had been made in Kentucky. At the coming of peace, the Indians knew that if they were to save their hunting grounds from the oncoming whites, they must strike before losing their British allies to the north.

All of Virginia had suffered great poverty—as had the other colonies during the hard years of the American Revolution. The soldiers had all been poorly clothed, fed, and paid. This being true, it is easy to understand why the Virginia government was slow to respond to the urgent demands of General George Rogers Clark, commander of the western troops, for ammunition, supplies, and pay for his armies, who were trying to defend this new county of Kentucky, the most western one of Virginia. There was dissatisfaction over the conditions—from Clark down to the last private. Mutiny was not uncommon. Many of the settlers returned to the more sheltered areas behind the Cumberlands; it took high courage to remain.

In August 1782, while Clark was busy defending Fort Nelson (Louisville), the settlers suffered their greatest defeat of the war at Blue Lick on the Licking River (Kentucky). Boone strongly advised against attacking the Indians there and lost his youngest son Israel in the engagement. Many minor defeats and atrocities occurred in that year, which caused Kentucky to be called "the dark and bloody ground."

Taught by the Blue Licks defeat, the people of Fayette and Lincoln counties at last awoke to the fatal consequences of discord; instead of refusing to join General Clark in a formidable expedition against the Indians, they were now anxious to have him take command. This he did.

He wrote to Harrison on October 24:

> It is planned and the rendezvous appointed for the mouth of the Licking the first day of November. I expect 1,000 men. If it is attended with success, I make

no doubt it will save the effusion of much blood the ensuing year.

In 1782, the soldier moved to Kennedy's Station, Kentucky and on October 1, ensuing enlisted and he served as private in Captain Adam's company, Colonel Benjamin Logan's regiment. They marched to the mouth of the Licking River, he was placed in Captain Wood's company, and they marched to the Shawnee towns under General Clark. He served five weeks in this expedition. With over a thousand men, Clark crossed the Ohio, marched rapidly against the principal Shawnee towns and destroyed them.

Samuel was one of the 1,000 men. He was twenty-one when he marched with Clark against the Shawnees, completing his service as a soldier of the revolution. No soldier should have been more proud of his supreme commander than he; no leader during the entire revolution displayed more sagacity, bravery, and determination than George Rogers Clark. In the face of hunger, mutiny, and insurmountable difficulties, he led his handful of impoverished men to victory in the capture of Vincennes, thereby saving the "Old Northwest" for the United States, which otherwise would have become part of Canada. So great was his generalship and his contribution to the ultimate defeat of the British, that had his service been recorded in just comparison of the events in the East, his record would stand out second-to-none in the annals of America's fight for freedom.

An old deed in Lebanon, county seat of Russell County, neighboring Scott County, shows that in 1806, John Alley and wife Mary Alley sold to Samuel Alley a good-sized tract of land on the north side of the Clinch River. This event was ten years after their marriage and it was quite likely that it was from this home that Samuel and Mary migrated to Indiana in 1810. He moved from Russell County, Virginia, to Brookville Township, Franklin County, Indiana. We have made much effort to find whether this John was Samuel's brother, but there is strong evidence that he was.

SAMUEL ALLEY

The year after Samuel and Mary were married, Samuel joined the Methodist Church. I'll let him tell of his experiences from the pages of his little book, which he wrote fifty-eight years later and had published for distribution to his family. These words are on the title page:

Christian Counsel

or

Error Reproved

By Samuel Alley, Sen.
Bloomington, Indiana,
S. H. Kredelbaugh, printer.
1846

PREFACE

This is to show in a concise manner, the cause of my writing to the Public.

In March 3, 1787, I set out publicly to serve God. At that time I lived in Washington County, Virginia. About that time the Methodist preachers came in to that country and I joined with them to serve the Lord. The preachers were humble, holy, loving men and preached free grace, which I always believed. I soon began to be acquainted with Mr. Wesley's writings, his discipline, rules, creed, and soon thought that he was almost infallible. Then I began to drink in a sectarian spirit—superstition and independence grew on. I thought we should soon take the world. I was made Class leader and when I had to turn out some loving souls that would weep at the door, I told this to the preachers and they said, "Let them weep on if they love their errors." This made a grievous wound in my heart not soon healed.

Notwithstanding, I remained with them, first and last, twelve or thirteen years. I received several permits to speak in public from the presiding elders. In this time I saw the spirit of division prevailing greatly and I saw the same spirit running through all sectarian religion. Then I remembered my covenant with the Lord—that I should always acknowledge the truth and deny error, up to the loss of life. I then made close examination of my heart and of the Scriptures, lest I should be in anything wrong. And this continued for the space of one year and six months.

> In this time I conferred not with flesh and blood. I then made public declaration of my views on the Gospel and reproved all error that I knew, and these errors I laid before the clergy of every sect occasionally as I had opportunity; them to examine and support, if they were able. But they would not support them or gainsay my sentiments. But the Methodist Bishops ordered me to Conference to be tried. One remarkable circumstance took place in Conference. The head of the board stood up with a loud voice and said, "Brethren, I want you to take notice that brother Sammy is not brought here to be tried for committing any sin or doing any evil, but only for a breach of our rules."
> Then I saw that he loved his rules more than the Gospel. I was not turned out at that Conference, but left with six months on trial, on condition that I must hold my tongue and say nothing about division or baptism. But I said that I would not hold my tongue when I saw that approbate division was the root of all error. I then reproved division and condemned it, renouncing everything that caused it. I then denied all sectarian names, creeds, rules, and disciplines and assumed the Christian name only—accepting only the creed and rules of the Bible. I then held up the Bible as a sufficient rule of faith and practice—the only rule to guide the world to Heaven.
> The year of my reformation was about 1798. I then saw delusion spreading through the world and thousands following the traditions of men. Is there any true ambassador of Christ who will keep silent? Therefore, be not offended at me for writing and trying to manifest the truth for the comfort and edification of a few followers of Christ; for the salvations of souls. Lord, send the truth like thunder!

Sounds pretty much like he brought that last sentence over from the Methodists! I added the exclamation point since I'm sure that he meant to say it with one.

Samuel Alley was a thinker as well as a fighter. He had fought for political freedom for himself and family, and now he was willing to fight for freedom of religious thought. Before joining the Methodists, he—without doubt—belonged to the Church of England or the Episcopal Church, as most of the Virginians did. To have become a Methodist, he had already discarded much of ritual and the formalities of the established church as he had known it. Now, where all was new, it seemed so natural that there should be freshness in the forms of worship.

In this new environment where all unnecessary equipment and hindering baggage had been cast aside, it seems so much in line that man-written dogmas and creeds hoary with age should be discarded, and only the Bible used.

CYRUS AND CHARITY NELSON

Cyrus was the third son and my great grandfather. He was a good man. My mother, as a child, was often at their home—and she loved her grandfather dearly. She often said to me that he should have married her grandmother Pumphrey; they were both so good and kind. He took his religion seriously, and though not an ordained minister, he often preached at nearby Christian churches when called. Cyrus was a farmer, and the house they lived in still stands, empty and uncared for.

Cyrus married Charity Nelson, daughter of Daniel and Ruth Nelson. Of her parents, I haven't been able to find any data. Tradition has it that Charity was a close relative (probably a niece) of Thomas Nelson, a signer of the Declaration of Independence. It is the accepted belief among all of the many descendants that this is true. I hope to sometime to do some research along this line. It is quite evident that there were some instances of aristocracy in her background and that she inherited some measure of it for being a close relative of Thomas Nelson.

I have so often heard my mother say, "Grandmother Charity was so aristocratic that I didn't like her as much as Grandfather Cyrus."

Mother spoke of her being so often dressed in her black silk with fine white apron and lace cap. She had money of her own or had a good way of extracting it from Great-Grandfather Cyrus; she promised to give $100 to each grandchild named for her! Now that was a wild promise; Cyrus and Charity had an even dozen children! And she kept her promise—except to one who named her offspring Charity Ruth and called her Ruth instead of Charity. Ha! Our great-grandmother was too smart to be fooled by that gesture; she just kept that $100.

After my Great-Grandfather Cyrus died, the grandchildren 'round about took turns staying with Grandmother Charity. They called her Granny Chat, whether to her face I don't know, but I doubt it. Out there on those dry, treeless plains in western Kansas, many were the tales that Mother would tell of her days with Granny Chat. She never failed to tell of the number of times a day that her grandmother would send her to the spring for "a fresh, cold drink."

I think Mother liked to live those times again in her fancies. When barefoot, she would play around the spring. She would usually end her story by saying, "How I'd love to see that old spot just once more and dip a drink from that old spring."

Well, she did get to do just that many, many years afterward when she and Father visited us in Indiana. Now, in 1950, I would so love to go back to the spot where the soddy stood when she told those tales to us! How many hallowed spots there are in this world to the folks who have passed the sixteenth milestone!

With all of her aristocratic notions, she was very superstitious and succeeded in filling the minds of the youngsters and my mother full of signs, witch tales, and ghost stories, but two of her grandsons beat her at her own game. Cyrus, her husband, was buried in the family cemetery not far away; at twilight, she would often sit at the window, watching and wondering if there were really ghosts that wandered about at dusk (dear old soul). one day when she was napping, those two rascally boys laid a line of black powder from their grandfather's grave up to her window. At dusk, when she was at her accustomed place, they slipped around to the grave and lit the line of powder. Their poor grandmother was frightened nearly out of her wits as the streak of fire came sputtering toward her! The one boy who had stayed in to witness the effect had to do some quick explaining!

Looking into the face on the little tintype, I imagine that I can see some austerity that may have called for a little evening up—perhaps, at least, some boys must have thought so. Mother, in her old grave, would chuckle every time she retold the tale, thinking it a good joke on Granny Chat.

The boys played another prank as I remember Mother telling. Her grandmother, being strict in her church attendance, one morning came down all dressed in her black silk and bonnet and told the boys to hurry in hitching the horse or she would be late to church. Grandmother had forgotten that yesterday was Sunday! They had wondered why she had not gone to church but had not inquired since it gave them one less chore to do. Should they tell her? No. They decided to hitch and let her go on and be fooled. After arriving at the closed church—with a little reckoning—she saw her mistake, but she was just too proud to admit it. When she drove in, she told the boys to unhitch and water the horse! She took some of the glint out of their glory all right.

THE BENEDICTION OF SAMUEL ALLEY

From a holy zeal and principle of love to my children, I have thought it prudent to leave with them my last dying counsel. And now my precious and beloved children (and your companions and children), give me your solemn attention in the fear of the Lord. You all know that I have done my duty as a Godly parent, raised you all tenderly and carefully, free from want, and in credit. In sickness I have used all tender diligence with the Lord's blessing for your recovery and comfort. I have prayed with you and for you day and night while reading the Bible, teaching you and admonishing you to serve the Lord, to seek Him early, and that He would be found of you.

I am shortly going to leave you all. I am very old and weak in body through afflictions. I am entirely dependent, being helpless, and now you bring down my gray hairs to the grave in sorrow by leaving me alone. I shall soon leave you all, but my prayers for you have never ceased. Consider what I say—you must have a good conscience; no man can stand before God with a guilty conscience. My dying counsel is for you to get the spirit of the Lord that bears the fruit of faith, love, and peace. I am both an elder and a father. I write not these things to get honor, but I desire that fruit may bound to your account.

Yet a little while and you will hear my voice no more. This only I desire, that your light and your fruit may be manifest before I die. That you are in the straight and narrow way, that I may have strong consolation, and that I may have good hope of meeting you in heaven. I must now bid you farewell and commend you to God and to the world of his grace that is able to build you up and give you an inheritance, along with all that are sanctified.